Trevor Wye
&
Patricia Morris

The Orchestral Flute Practice
Book 2

NOVELLO PUBLISHING LIMITED
8-9 Frith Street, London W1V 5TZ

With thanks to the Librarians of the BBC Symphony Orchestra
for their unfailing support, patience and kindness

Exclusive distributors:
MUSIC SALES LIMITED
Newmarket Road,
Bury St Edmunds,
Suffolk IP33 3YB.
All rights reserved.

Order No. NOV120802
ISBN 0-85360-807-5
© Copyright 1998 Novello & Company Limited.
8-9 Frith Street, London W1V 5TZ.

Music processed by Barnes Music Engraving.
Book design by Pearce Marchbank, Studio Twenty.
Printed in the United Kingdom by
Redwood Books, Trowbridge, Wiltshire

CONTENTS

PREFACE

It has always struck us as odd that in conservatories and colleges of music throughout the world, we learn the repertoire for flute and piano much more thoroughly than the orchestral repertoire. Yet professionally, very, very few flute players are able to support themselves as soloists. Of course, the repertoire for flute and piano is more self-contained and therefore more satisfying to practise. So, in order to encourage the would-be orchestral player to work at these extracts regularly, we have presented the important solos with 'cue lines' to help them understand the 'background'. We hope our efforts will help important solos come alive.

Try as we might, we couldn't begin to compile the complete orchestral vade mecum because, even as you are reading this, more is being written! All the same, these two volumes contain a large proportion of the major orchestral material that a player will encounter, as well as some they are unlikely to play! Times and fashions change for composers, too: orchestral managers, conductors and impresarios all have their current favourite repertoire and what may be an important orchestral work today could be forgotten tomorrow. So with that in mind, we have included all the major orchestral repertoire and in addition we have included some which were once popular and could reappear.

Many passages which are not 'solo' in the real sense of the word are also included, because we are sure you will be grateful for a look at the notes before the first rehearsal. Some lesser known solos are included to enable you to consider musical style and the use of different tone colours which are available in the flute's palette.

Cue lines have been included as a guide and a reminder as to what else is happening in the orchestra during the big moment. However helpful this cue line may prove, it can't replace a look at the score. If you haven't played it or heard it before try to listen to a recording, though it doesn't take the place of real orchestral experience. If at all possible, listen with the score so that you'll have some sense of the whole piece into which the solo fits. The cue lines have been transposed into 'C' in the treble clef, to facilitate easier reference. (In doing this, relative octaves have been ignored.)

This book is divided into 5 sections, each of which features specific orchestral or sectional problems. The last is a general section, which covers the remaining standard repertoire you need to cover. Volume 1 covers composers A to M; Volume 2 features N to Z. Where possible, we have tried to keep all the excerpts from one work together in the same section, to make practising easier. However, where works contain specific examples of orchestral difficulties, we have grouped these together so that a particular aspect of orchestral playing can be focused on and studied.

WHERE TO START

There is a lot of music in these two volumes, and to be realistic - because of individual preferences of both conductors and orchestral managements - some of it you may never play. We suggest you start with the most popular ones in the list THE TOP TWENTY-EIGHT (see Volume 1, page 5). If you have any major technical difficulties such as articulation, playing softly in the third octave, or fingering problems, then we recommend that you work firstly with appropriate material such as articulation exercises or tone studies*. The reason for this is that if you practise an orchestral passage purely as an exercise, you are likely to play it like that in an orchestra, losing its interest and vitality. So remove any major problems with suitable exercises, and then these extracts shouldn't be too problematic.

Practise memorising the big tunes in different keys where that is possible. On returning to the original key, one often finds more flexibility and freedom of expression than before (advice which Marcel Moyse advocated when learning a difficult or important solo). Try to include an orchestral excerpt each day as a part of your practise routine, rather than having a periodic burst at half a dozen. In addition, it's valuable to work at a contemporary extract as part of your daily schedule. Some of the more common and harmonically simple extracts should be memorised, such as the Mendelssohn 'Scherzo' and 'L'après midi d'un faune'. That will allow you to try them out at any time and place, perhaps as warm-ups, without getting the book out to practise.

* Trevor Wye's Practice Books For The Flute Volumes 1 to 6 (Novello)

TOP OF THE POPS

Recent surveys of orchestral audition lists have revealed the popularity of some pieces which we have called 'Top of The Pops'. Of course, fashions change in orchestral concert planning and a number of people are involved in selecting audition pieces: the leader, the conductor, the orchestral management and the flute section. A good indication of what might be given as sight-reading is a look at the recent programmes of the orchestra for which you are auditioning.

This list is approximately in order of international audition popularity at the time of writing, and there is no reason to expect it to change very much in the forseeable future. It goes without saying that the top twenty-eight should be thoroughly learned - not just for the upcoming audition, but as a future investment:. To have these pieces tucked in your belt is to be well prepared.

THE TOP TWENTY-EIGHT
According to popularity:

1	Ravel	DAPHNIS ET CHLOÉ
2	Debussy	PRÉLUDE À L'APRÈS MIDI D'UN FAUNE
3	Beethoven	OVERTURE: LEONORE No.3
4	Mendelssohn	SCHERZO from A MIDSUMMER NIGHT'S DREAM
5	Brahms	SYMPHONY No.4
6	Prokofiev	CLASSICAL SYMPHONY
7	R Strauss	TILL EULENSPIEGELS
8	Prokofiev	PETER AND THE WOLF
9	Saint-Saëns	VOLIERE from CARNIVAL OF THE ANIMALS
10	Tchaikovsky	SYMPHONY No.4
11	Dvořák	SYMPHONY IN G MAJOR
12	Bartók	CONCERTO FOR ORCHESTRA
13	Rimsky-Korsakov	SHEHERAZADE
14	Stravinsky	PETROUCHKA
15	Berlioz	SYMPHONIE FANTASTIQUE
16	Brahms	SYMPHONY No.1
17	Beethoven	SYMPHONY No.3
18	Stravinsky	FIREBIRD SUITE
19	Stravinsky	SONG OF THE NIGHTINGALE
20	Hindemith	SYMPHONIC METAMORPHOSES
21	Britten	SEA INTERLUDES
22	R Strauss	SALOME
23	Bizet	ENTR'ACTE from CARMEN
24	Prokofiev	LIEUTENANT KIJÉ
25	Prokofiev	ROMEO AND JULIET
26	Ravel	BOLERO*
27	Rossini	'WILLIAM TELL' OVERTURE
28	JS Bach	No.58 FROM THE ST MATTHEW PASSION

* No extracts from this work are included in these volumes.

ALSO LIKELY TO APPEAR
In alphabetical order:

JS Bach	ST. JOHN PASSION
Beethoven	SYMPHONIES Nos.1, 6 & 7
Borodin	POLOTSVIAN DANCES
Brahms	SYMPHONY No.3
Britten	THE YOUNG PERSON'S GUIDE TO THE ORCHESTRA
Debussy	LA MER
	NOCTURNES
Dvořák	'NEW WORLD' SYMPHONY
Gluck	DANCE OF THE BLESSED SPIRITS
	from ORFEO ED EURIDICE
Kodály	PEACOCK VARIATIONS
Mahler	DAS LIED VON DER ERDE (last movement)
Mendelssohn	SYMPHONY No.4
Musorgsky	NIGHT ON THE BARE MOUNTAIN
Piston	THE INCREDIBLE FLUTIST
Prokofiev	SYMPHONY No.5
Ravel	MOTHER GOOSE SUITE
	LA VALSE
Reznicek	DONNA DIANA OVERTURE
Rimsky-Korsakov	CAPRICCIO ESPAGNOLE
	RUSSIAN EASTER OVERTURE
Rossini	THE BARBER OF SEVILLE
	OVERTURES (various)
	SEMIRAMIDE
Schubert	SYMPHONIES Nos.5 & 9
Schumann	SYMPHONY No.1
Shostakovich	SYMPHONIES Nos.1, 5, 6, 10, & 15
Smetana	THE BARTERED BRIDE OVERTURE
R Strauss	EIN HELDENLEBEN
	SYMPHONIA DOMESTICA
Stravinsky	DUMBARTON OAKS
	THE FAIRY'S KISS
	THE RITE OF SPRING
	SONG OF THE NIGHTINGALE
	SYMPHONY IN 3 MOVEMENTS
Tchaikovsky	THE NUTCRACKER SUITE
	PIANO CONCERTO No.1 (second movement)
	SYMPHONY No.6
Thomas	MIGNON OVERTURE
Wagner	MAGIC FIRE MUSIC

THE AUDITION

The orchestral management advertises and you reply: by doing so, you are implying that you are just the person they are looking for! A time and place for your audition is agreed upon and from that moment, it's your responsibility to prove it.

Prepare yourself properly. If you are relatively (or even completely) inexperienced, it's not enough to simply learn the notes. You need to know how your part fits into the accompanying orchestral texture, and you must reflect this knowledge in your performance of the passage. Always take a piccolo; the principal player is sometimes required to change to the piccolo, and a reasonable ability on it is usually a requirement. If you have arrived early, don't be put off by what you can hear of the person already in mid-audition. Everyone sounds good through closed doors!

Rhythm is the most important point to remember about any sight-reading you may be given. This is especially critical in long notes and trills - it's so easy to lose track of the beat. Keep all long notes for their full value, even if exceptionally long. If you are given what is in fact 'real' sight-reading (something you have never seen before) concentrate on the correct rhythm as well as the right notes. Look upon rhythm as a priority. In an orchestra, if you were to play a rhythm incorrectly (and that includes miscounting rests or long notes) or enter in the wrong place, you may well upset someone else's entry who has been following your cue in their part.

Your solo with piano: unless you take your own pianist to the audition, you will have to rely on the staff pianist engaged by the orchestral management. These accompanists are usually (but not always) competent; normally there is no rehearsal so you will only have a few seconds to discuss tempi, etc. The accompanist may or may not be familiar with your solo, so to be on the safe side, don't choose a piece with a really difficult piano part or one which they are unlikely to know . You will probably feel more secure in your musical performance if you take your own pianist with whom you have rehearsed.

Sometimes the panel specify the solo, sometimes not. If you have a free choice, the most usual solos are the Mozart Concerti (one of which is normally specified), the Ibert and Nielsen Concerti and the Prokofiev Sonata. Other frequently played pieces are the works of Hüe, Fauré, Enesco, Dutilleux, Messiaen, Poulenc, Bozza, Gaubert, Ibert ('Pièce'), Martin and Widor. If you are asked to choose two contrasting pieces, you should choose one classical piece to show your sense of style plus a modern or Romantic piece to show off your variety of tone colours and virtuosity. Your choice must demonstrate what you are capable of!

If you are auditioning for a second flute position, how would you approach your solo? Do you play the Prokofiev Flute Sonata like a second flautist? No, but you can reflect in your performance the attributes of a good second flute player. For example, a good, firm, in-tune low register would help, as would the ability to play very softly and in tune with a varied vibrato. Musical sensitivity, a sense of the style of different periods, and attention paid to dynamics, accents, lengths of notes and articulation would all be suggestive of flexibility in a positive way. A big-toned aggressive performance probably wouldn't be advantageous; the principal player wants a colleague who will support them and fit in with the section, not someone who is overly ambitious and wishing they were in the principal's job! An inflexible and heavy vibrato would also be a disadvantage.

'The orchestra obviously wants someone who is experienced... But how do I become experienced if I can't get a job in the first place?' This is a question frequently asked by students. You can accomplish a great deal by concert going, by taking on the meanest work just for the experience, and by listening frequently to the radio and to recordings. Don't pass up the opportunity to play any kind of chamber music, or indeed flute duets, trios or quartets. These can be a fruitful ground for ensemble and intonation practice. Marcel Moyse once said that flute duets were his only orchestral experience until he joined an orchestra.

IMPOSSIBLE TRILLS

There are a few instances of 'impossible' trills in the repertoire, such as between low C and C♯, but even these can be judiciously 'arranged' so that they become possible! The trill between low C to C♯, for example, can be played by using the inside of your right knee to hold down the C♯ key. It's then simple to trill with just the C lever! The same trick can be accomplished with the trill from C♯ to D♯. With two or more players in the section, the parts can be swopped around so that the player on the right of the 'impossible trill' can play one-handed whilst holding down a key on the flute to their left (provided this is out of sight of the audience!). Alternatively, the use of an elastic band to temporarily hold down a key can get you out of trouble. There is usually some way around an impossible trill. (A full list of trills with alternatives can be found elsewhere.*)

DIFFICULT PASSAGES

A few composers have written passages without being informed about the problems of actually playing them! A good orchestral player will be aware of possible alternative fingering; using harmonics, for example. It would be wise to familiarise yourself with these if you haven't already done so. Start on low C and, using the second harmonic (or overtone), play a chromatic scale. Apart from the first four notes, the rest are all the same as the usual fingering in the second octave. Now repeat this scale using the third harmonic as the starting note. Follow this by using the fourth and fifth harmonics as starting notes. As you go higher up, the number of notes becomes more restricted, but these notes can sometimes get you out of trouble.

You aren't using the correct fingering? There is no such thing. The correct fingering is the one that gives the best and smoothest result. The orchestral position will go to the most competent player - not necessarily to the one who fingers the flute according to the fingering chart.

* Trevor Wye's Practice Book For The Flute Volume 6 (NOV120591)

Section One

THE MIDDLE AND UPPER REGISTER

Towards a fine even cantabile

A beautiful singing tone was probably what attracted you to the flute in the first place. These extracts were written to exploit this particular attribute, using the most lovely part of the flute's compass: the middle to high register.

See also:

Berlioz	Symphonie Fantastique	General Section, Book 1
Brahms	Symphony No. 2	General Section, Book 1
Mahler	Symphony No. 9	Section 4, Book 2
Prokofiev	Peter and the Wolf	Section 2, Book 1
Rimsky-Korsakov	Sheherazade	General Section, Book 2
Schubert	Symphony No. 8 (Unfinished)	General Section, Book 2
J. Strauss	Die Fledermaus	General Section, Book 2

SYMPHONY NO. 6, 'PASTORAL'

1st Movement

A happy 'pastoral' tone is required, for which you need to learn to project the sound without forcing it.

BEETHOVEN

2nd Movement

(Nightingale)

3rd Movement

4th Movement

5th Movement

BENVENUTO CELLINI

Overture

(Paris 2, Weimar version)

BERLIOZ

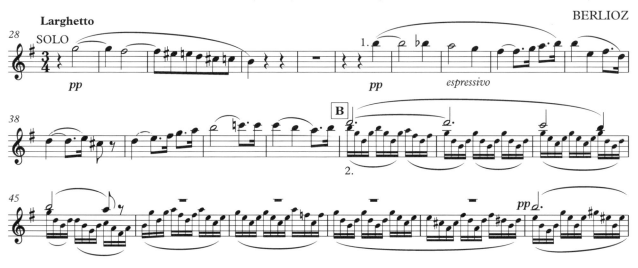

SYMPHONY NO. 6

1st Movement

Ruhig: quiet and peaceful.

BRUCKNER

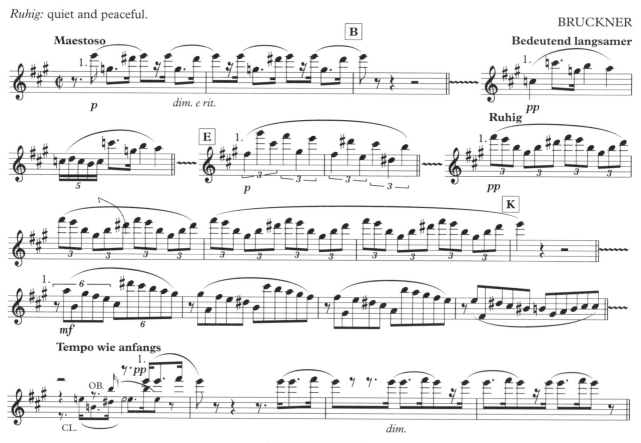

BRIGG FAIR

Delius' use of the flute is rather special. The style of playing should reflect his soft, gentle, unfocussed scoring.

DELIUS

13

SYMPHONY NO. 7

2nd Movement

DVOŘÁK

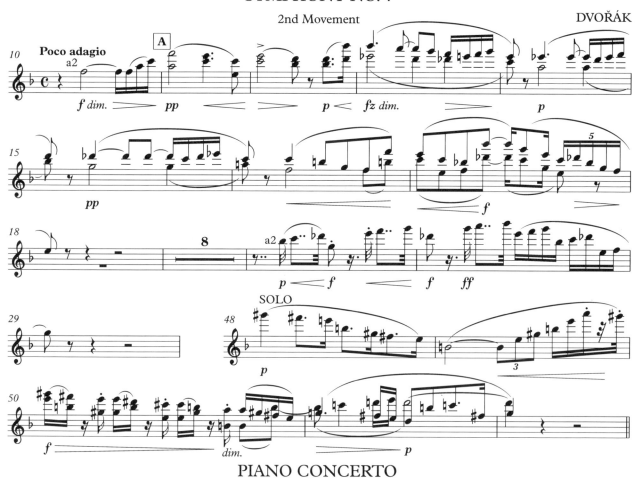

PIANO CONCERTO

3rd Movement

If you have any difficulty placing the triplets you may wish to experiment with the advice offered by Quantz: if you want triplets to sound more like triplets, lengthen the first two notes of each group.

The turn at the end of this passage reintroduces the piano.

GRIEG

PEER GYNT SUITE

1. Morning

GRIEG

THE MAGIC FLUTE

Overture

In the *Allegro*, try to be aware of the other parts as you play the solos.

MOZART

No. 8 Act 1, Finale

'Wie stark ist nicht dein Zauberton'

The appoggiaturas (bar 175 onwards) are usually played as a semiquaver on the beat.

NIGHT ON A BARE MOUNTAIN

The ornament in bar 2 is usually played before the beat.

MUSORGSKY arr. RIMSKY-KORSAKOV

DAPHNIS ET CHLOÉ

Introduction et Danse Religieuse

RAVEL

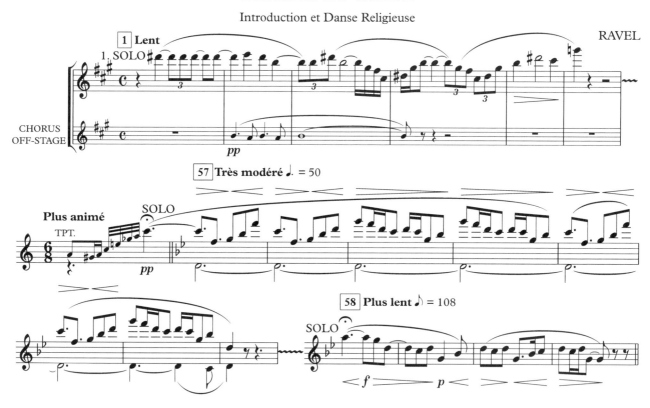

THE SILKEN LADDER

(La scala di seta)

Overture

ROSSINI

PIANO CONCERTO

In A minor

1st Movement

SCHUMANN

Section Two

CADENZAS

Cadenzas are inserted to excite and delight the audience, to illustrate or comment on an event in the piece, or simply to link one section to another. A cadenza should sound as though it is being created at the moment of performance and should never sound dull or predictable.

In some cadenzas the conductor will indicate a tempo, but usually they will leave you to do your own thing. Though you may be free to use your imagination, do respect the relationship of the different rhythms to each other to preserve the composer's general idea of tempo.

The Strauss example is a particularly difficult one because it is so naïve and doesn't change key. It is a challenge to the player to create something beautiful out of what amounts to a few trills and arpeggios. They are in any case, good practice.

Many other extracts in these two volumes contain cadenzas:

Bartók	Concerto for Orchestra	Section 2, Book 1
Bernstein	West Side Story	General Section, Book 1
Delibes	Coppélia	General Section, Book 1
Hindemith	Harmonie der Welt	General Section, Book 1
Mahler	Symphony No. 2	Section 4, Book 2
Rimsky Korsakov	Capriccio Espagnol	General Section, Book 2
Stravinsky	Song of the Nightingale	General Section, Book 2
	The Firebird Suite	General Section, Book 2
	The Fairy's Kiss	General Section, Book 2
Thomas	Mignon Overture	General Section, Book 2
Vaughan Williams	Symphony No. 4	General Section, Book 2

EASTER OVERTURE

RIMSKY-KORSAKOV

TALES FROM THE VIENNA WOODS

STRAUSS

SYMPHONY NO. 1

4th Movement

SCHUMANN

Section Three

ORCHESTRAL DUETS AND TRIOS

An important section to practise with your friends. The major points to watch out for are intonation, balance between parts, and matching your tone with the other players. The second and third players should familiarise themselves with the first part to be able to match up dynamics and note lengths at the first rehearsal. In the Liszt and Wagner excerpts, practising the three parts together can be particularly beneficial. Be aware of intonation, matching your tone, unanimity of dynamics, attack and length of notes, and awareness of the speed and amount of vibrato.

See also:

Bartók	Concerto for Orchestra	Section 2, Book 1
	The Miraculous Mandarin	General Section, Book 1
	Duke Bluebeard's Castle	General Section, Book 1
Bax	The Garden of Fand	General Section, Book 1
Brahms	Variations on a Theme by Haydn	General Section, Book 1
Debussy	Prélude à l'après midi d'un faune	Section 2, Book 1
Delius	Brigg Fair	Section 1, Book 2
Haydn	The Creation	Section 6, Book 1
Maxwell Davies	Symphony No. 2	Section 5, Book 2
Mendelssohn	A Midsummer Night's Dream	General Section, Book 1
	Calm Sea and Prosperous Voyage Overture	General Section, Book 1
Prokofiev	Classical Symphony	General Section, Book 1
Rachmaninov	Rhapsody on a Theme of Paganini	General Section, Book 2
Ravel	Daphnis et Chloé	General Section, Book 2
Shostakovich	Symphony No. 7 (3rd movt)	General Section, Book 2
Stravinsky	The Firebird Suite	General Section, Book 2
Tchaikovsky	Nutcracker Suite: Danse des Mirlitons	General Section, Book 2
	Suite No. 3	General Section, Book 2

ST MATTHEW PASSION

5. Recitativo: Du lieber Heiland du

Like much of Bach's music, the solos and duets usually lack dynamic markings; these should be included to reflect the direction of both the melody and the harmony.

JS BACH

Gra - be will be - rei - ten, so las - se mir in - zwi - schen zu, von mei - ner

Au - gen Trä - nen - flüs - sen ein Was - ser __ auf __ dein Haupt zu gie - ßen!

6. Aria: Buß und Reu

The ornament in bar 4 is usually played as a quaver.

Buß __ und Reu, Buß __ und Reu knirscht das __

Sün - den - herz ent - zwei;

Buß __ und Reu, __ Buß __ und Reu __ knirscht __ das

Sün - den - herz ent - zwei, knirscht_ das Sün - den - herz ent - zwei, Buß und_ Reu,_

Buß und_ Reu_ knirscht das Sün - den - herz ent - zwei, Buß_____ und

Reu_ knirscht das_ Sün - den - herz ent - zwei,

daß die Trop - fen mei - ner Zäh - ren an - ge - neh - me Spe - ze - rei,_____

_ treu - er_ Je - su,_ dir_ ge - bä - ren;

daß die Trop - fen mei - ner_ Zäh - ren an - ge - neh - me_____ Spe - ze - rei,

19. Recitativo: O Schmerz!

MASS IN B MINOR

KYRIE

1. Kyrie eleison

JS BACH

MAGNIFICAT

9. Esurientes implevit bonis

JS BACH

-a - nes, di-mi-sit in-a - nes;

e - su - ri - en - tes im - ple - vit_ bo - nis, e -

bo - nis et di - vi - tes_ di - mi - sit, et di - vi - tes_ di - mi - sit, di - mi - sit

in - a - nes, di-mi-sit in - a - nes, di-mi-sit in-a - nes.

12. Gloria patri

L'ENFANCE DU CHRIST

Part 1. Le Songe d'Hérode

Scene VI: Les Anges Invisibles, Marie et Joseph

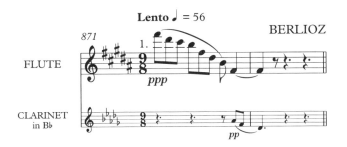

Dance of the Ishmaélites

from Part 3. (The Arrival at Sais)

Scene II

*If necessary, a breath can be taken here, and in similar places throughout.

L'ARLÉSIENNE

Suite No. 1

II. Minuetto

BIZET

Andantino (♩. = 54)   IV. Carillon

THE YOUNG PERSON'S GUIDE TO THE ORCHESTRA

The small notes are to be played if the commentary is not spoken; this is usually the case and provides a very tricky passage, especially the second flute entries.

Variation A

BRITTEN

VARIATIONS ON A HUNGARIAN FOLKSONG

(The Peacock)

Variation II

KODÁLY

Con brio ♩ = 104

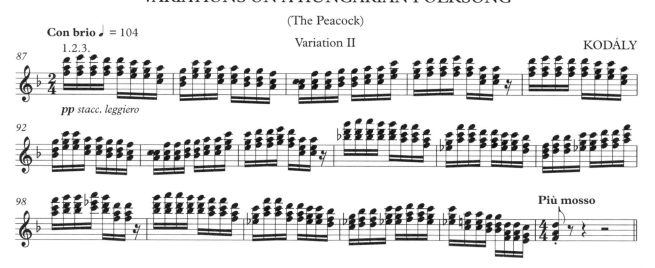

Variation IX

This is for two flutes and two clarinets; a look at the score would be helpful.

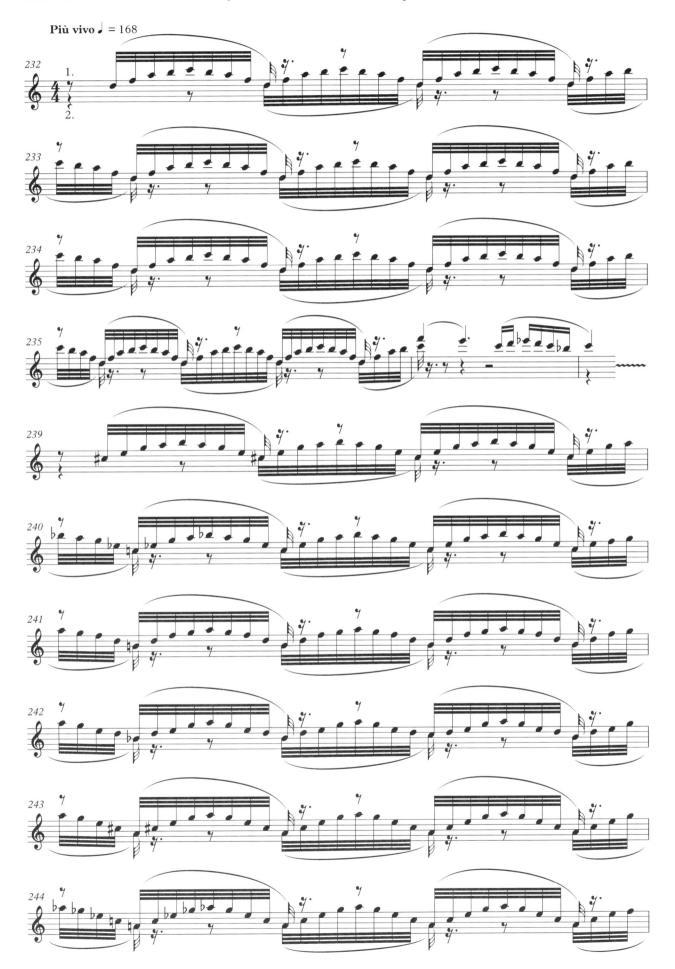

Variation XIV

The first section of this variation is a solo accompanied by strings and harp.

Finale

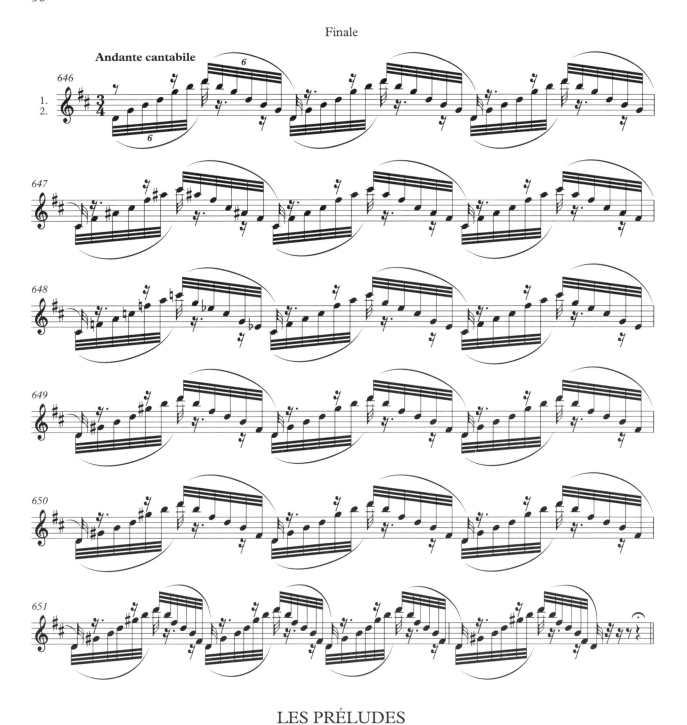

LES PRÉLUDES

This should be practised by the whole wind section together but getting the flutes in tune will help.

LISZT

SYMPHONY NO. 4

(The Italian)

1st Movement

MENDELSSOHN

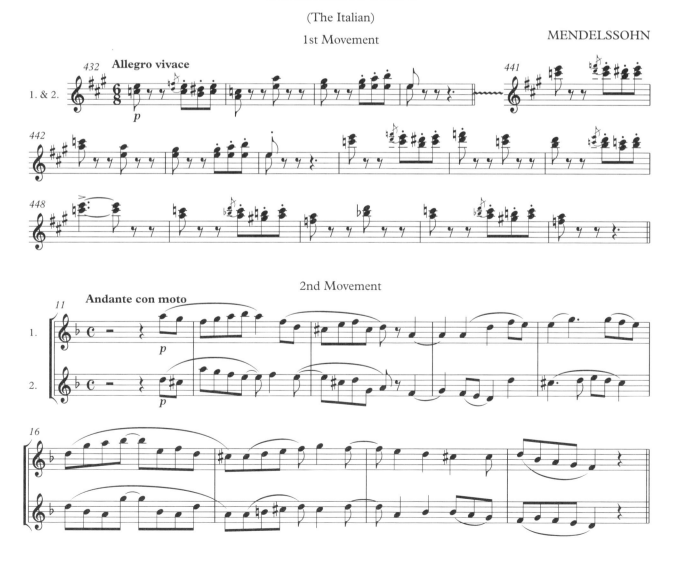

4th Movement

A MIDSUMMER NIGHT'S DREAM

Overture

This opening is notorious for intonation problems. To sound 'correct', the major thirds should be flattened.

MENDELSSOHN

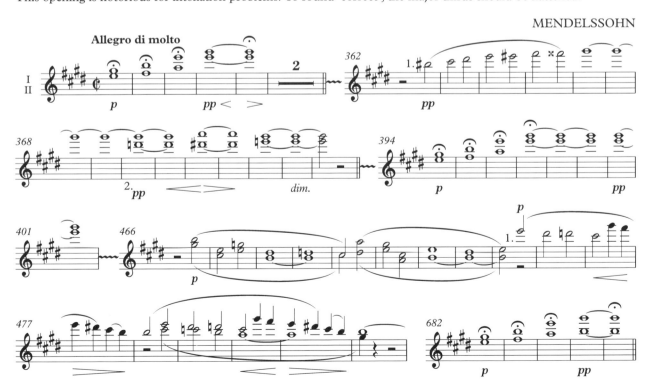

SYMPHONY NO. 2

4th Movement – Finale

SIBELIUS

MÁ VLAST

2. Vltava

(The Moldau)

The two players should aim for a uniform match of tone and dynamic.

SMETANA

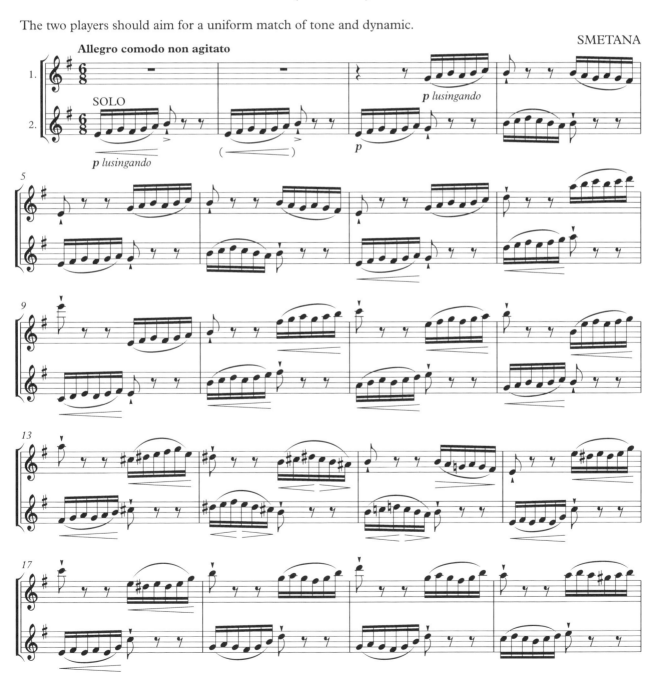

Village Wedding

Moonlight; Dance of the Nymphs

L'OISEAU DE FEU

(The Firebird: Suite)

Introduction

STRAVINSKY

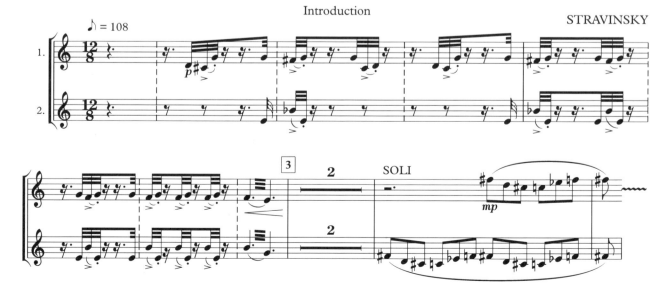

L'oiseau de feu et sa danse ♩ = 132

Variation de l'oiseau de feu ♩ = 76

ROMEO AND JULIET

Fantasy Overture

This short passage creates intonation problems for the whole wind section. Make sure you have corrected your own problems, so that you are able to be flexible in the section.

TCHAIKOVSKY

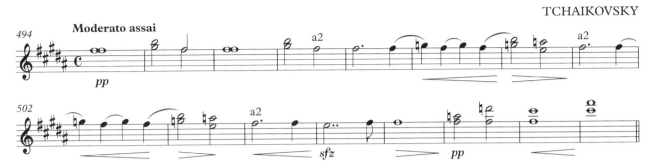

LOHENGRIN

Prelude

Practise these passages together as a section.

WAGNER

PARSIFAL

Prelude

WAGNER

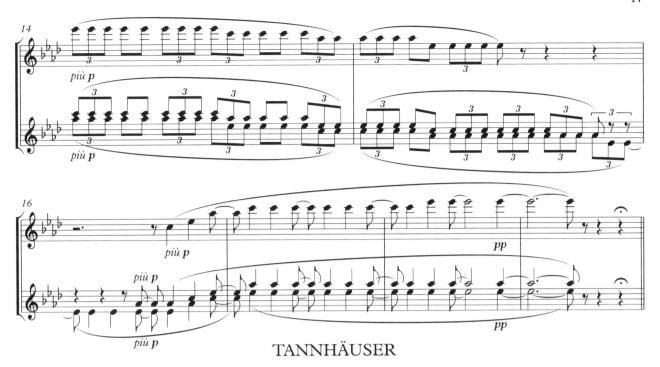

TANNHÄUSER

Act 3. Gebet der Elisabeth

(Elisabeth's prayer)

WAGNER

Section Four

THE AUSTRO-GERMAN SCHOOL

MAHLER'S WORKS

Mahler's directions, sprinkled liberally throughout the score, demand either a reasonable knowledge of German, or at least some time spent with a dictionary in order to know what is going to happen. We have appended a list of the most commonly-used directions, including those in the pieces in this book. You would be wise to read and observe these instructions for an audition.

Regarding the style: take care of the little notes in a phrase – do not allow them to become passing notes. A shimmery French tone and vibrato is inappropriate in this music, which demands a darker and heavier colour. You will often be part of a block of sound with the rest of the woodwind, like an organ. In such passages, over-use of vibrato will not blend with the rest of the section.

allmählich	gradually
(mit) Ausdruck	(with) expression, expressive
bedeutend	meaningful
beruhigen	calm down, gradually get slower/calmer
beruhigend	soothing
bewegt(er)	(more) movement, motion – più mosso
Bewegung	movement, motion
etwas	some/somewhat
dieser/diese/dieses	this
drängend	pressing, pushing, urging
doppelt so schnell	twice as fast
duftig	delicate, fragrant (der Duft = the fragrance)
(mit) durchaus ernstem und festlichem Ausdruck	with completely serious/earnest and festive expression
eilen (nicht)	(do not) rush
ein wenig fließender, doch immer langsam	a little more flowing, but always slow
etwas frischer	somewhat more fresh/lively
feierlich	festive/solemn
festes Zeitmaß	steady tempo
fließend(er)	(more) flowing
flüchtig	cursory
frisch(er)	(more) fresh/lively
früheres Tempo	earlier tempo
früheres Zeitmaß	earlier tempo
galant	gallant, courteous
ganz	wholly
gehalten	held back (usually refers to the tempo: rather slow)
gemächlich	leisurely
spielen/gespielt	to play/played
heftig	fierce, violent
hervortretend	projecting, prominent
h-Fuß	B-foot
immer	always
im Tempo eines gemächlichen Ländlers	in the tempo of a leisurely 'Ländler' (country dance)
in diesem Wetter!	in this weather!
langsam(er)	slow(er)
lebhaft	lively
leicht	light, easy
leise	quiet, soft
mäßig	moderate
mäßiges Zeitmaß	moderate tempo
mit Wut	with anger/rage/fury
Nachtmusik	night music
nicht	not
nicht zu schnell	not too fast
ohne	without
ohne Nachschlag	without turn (at the end of a trill)
plötzlich	suddenly/subito

ritterlich	knightly, chivalrous
ruhelos	restless
ruhig(er)	calm(er)
schleppen(d)	drag(ging)
scharf und spitzig	sharp and pointed
schmerzvoll	painful
schnell(er)	fast(er)
sehr	very
sich	oneself
sehr trotzig	very defiant
stetig	constant, continual
steigern	increase
unruhig	restless/fidgety
(sich) verlierend	losing, disappearing
Vogelstimme	birdsong
wie	like, as
wieder	again
Wiegenlied	lullaby/cradle song
wie vorher	as before
wie früher	as before/earlier
wieder langsam	slowly again
zart	soft
ziemlich	quite
zögernd	hesitant
zurückhaltend (etwas)	(somewhat) reserved/held back
zurückhalten	to hold back/reserve

SYMPHONY NO. 7

1st Movement

BRUCKNER

2nd Movement

50

3rd Movement

Trio

SYMPHONY NO. 8 (1890 version)

4th Movement

BRUCKNER

SYMPHONY NO. 9

2nd Movement: Scherzo

BRUCKNER

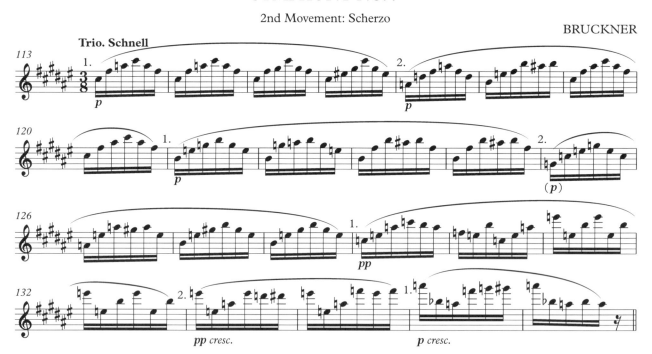

SYMPHONY NO. 2

1st Movement

MAHLER

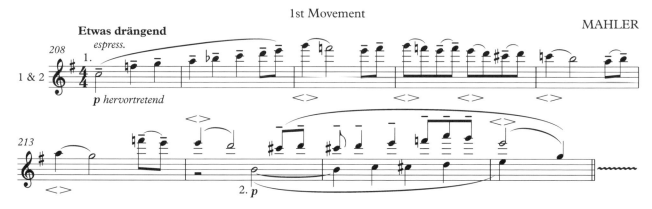

3rd Movement

21 **In ruhig fliessender Bewegung**

5th Movement

SYMPHONY NO. 5

1st Movement

MAHLER

3rd Movement

5th Movement

SYMPHONY NO. 7

2nd Movement: Nachtmusik

MAHLER

Andante amoroso

4th Movement: Nachtmusik II

SYMPHONY NO. 8

1st Part. Hymn: Veni, creator spiritus

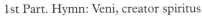

MAHLER

Allegro impetuoso
Sehr zart und gehalten

SYMPHONY NO. 9

1st Movement

MAHLER

*See page ???

SYMPHONY NO. 10

5th Movement: Finale

MAHLER
(Finished version
prepared by Deryck Cooke)

DAS KLAGENDE LIED

I. Sehr gehalten

MAHLER

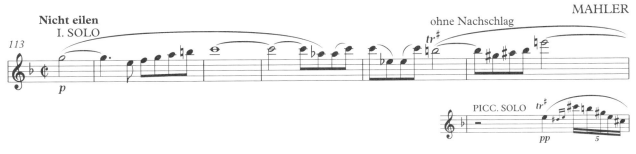

KINDERTOTENLIEDER

5. In diesem Wetter!

At 'Stetig steigernd', note the similarity to Dvořák's Symphony in G major where notes in the same harmonic series cause a simple passage to be problematic.

These examples are included to illustrate the difficulties of Richard Strauss' orchestral works. The majority of his works will require study prior to performing them.

EIN HELDENLEBEN

R. STRAUSS

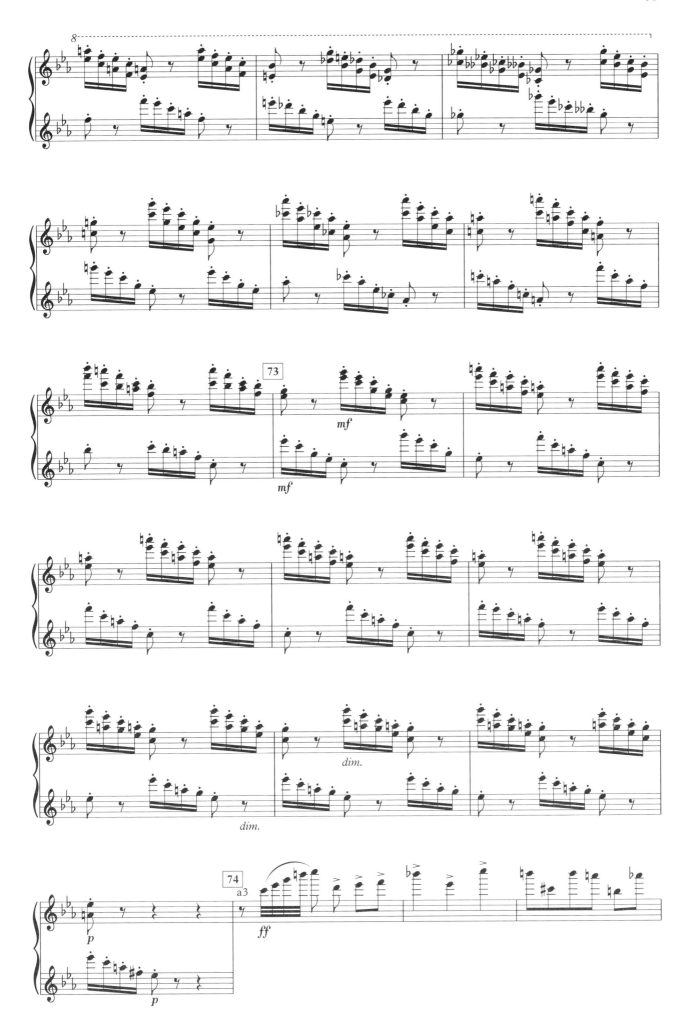

LE BOURGEOIS GENTILHOMME

Der Bürger als Edelmann

II. Menuet

R. STRAUSS

VIII.

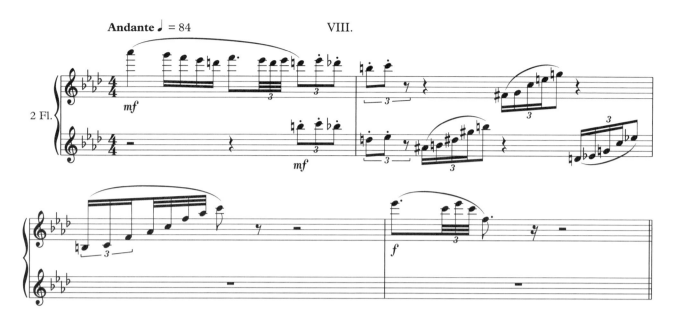

IX.

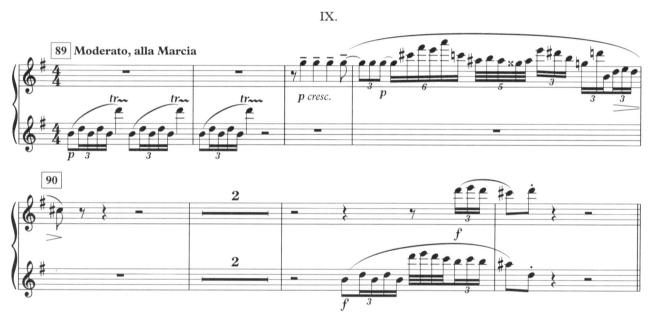

SYMPHONIA DOMESTICA

R. STRAUSS

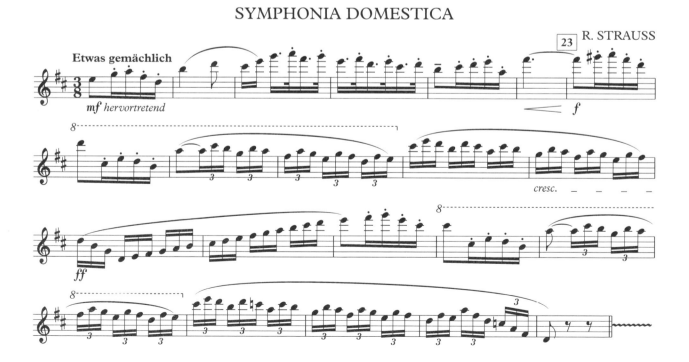

Section Five

CONTEMPORARY ORCHESTRAL WRITING

In this section, we've included examples of different styles of writing, quoting a selection of composers. Contemporary music can be very diverse as our selection will show. You can see that the flute is used to add a large variety of colours to the complex textures created by the composers. This demands many different techniques including playing notes of indeterminate pitch, using exotic rhythms, producing sounds of no pitch, banging the fingers down without blowing, playing 'air only' sounds and playing chords. There are also the more common devices such as flutter tonguing, *glissandi*, bending notes and quarter tones, to name but a few! These techniques, only briefly encountered in mainstream solo repertoire, are frequently found in this music. It is essential to get the part in advance.

This selection is only a guide to the styles, not in any way a comprehensive list. New contemporary pieces are being created all the time. It is impractical to do other than present a selection of typical works which demonstrate this constantly changing genre.

Hints on the more common techniques:

FLUTTER TONGUING: There are examples of this in the Berg, Berio and Webern. Producing an effective flutter at the right moment is a question of choosing which kind (the throat or with the rolled r's) and practising its extension into both extremes of the flute's compass. The less the lips move when fluttering, the more successful it seems to be. Experiment with the speed of the roll – a slower speed is often better. To get it to start – especially *piano* – is the tricky part. Have the airstream ready, with no sudden explosion of air, and consider beginning with a 'pe' syllable.

HARMONICS: A circle above a note generally indicates the use of an harmonic or overtone. Some composers indicate the specific fundamental on which the harmonic is to be produced, in which case the required note has the fundamental written directly underneath as a diamond shaped note. Other composers indicate a harmonic but are not specific. This may mean that they want a thin, inexpressive sound rather like the violin's harmonics, in which case there are special fingerings for these soft notes. The player has to decide which fingering to use depending on the underlying harmony. Most of the special fingered notes are sharp and need to be tested first.

GLISSANDI: When making a glissando from, for example, B to D downwards in the middle register, hold the upper note for almost its full value first before beginning your descent. As you slide down, diminish the volume during the descent; and finally, don't try to play a complete chromatic scale – it usually isn't necessary. When going up, the same remarks apply except that the open holes on your flute can help by sliding one or two fingers off on the way.

RHYTHMS: Complicated time signatures or complex rhythmic patterns can only be played fluently after learning them accurately first. As we become accustomed to this style, so it becomes easier to 'sight-read' them. We recommend that you work at a piece from this section regularly, particularly if you are completely unfamiliar with contemporary music style. Time signatures are not always as complex as they first appear, and the use of special symbols is recommended for easier reading later.

KAMMERKONZERT

BERG

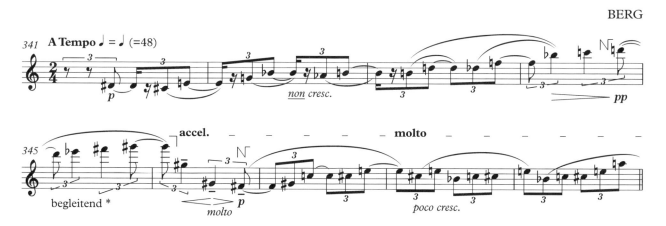

VIOLIN CONCERTO

1st Movement

BERG

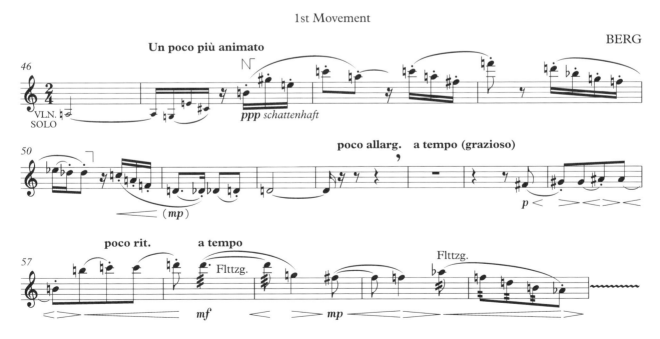

N⌐ Nebenstimme

H⌐ Hauptstimme

⌐ this section is played in the same rhythm as a Haupt- or Nebenstimme

LABORINTUS II

BERIO

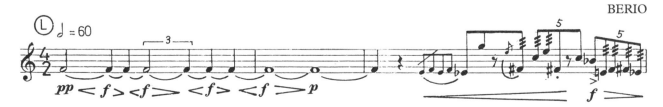

NOMOS

BIRTWISTLE

↓sign indicates grace-notes to be played on the beat
*These dynamics take place within an overall diminuendo (*mp* to *pppp*)

RITUEL

in memoriam bruno maderna

As with the first extract given here, all these passages move in the same peculiar style of groups (three flutes and drum) playing together but each set off in a random way by the conductor.

BOULEZ

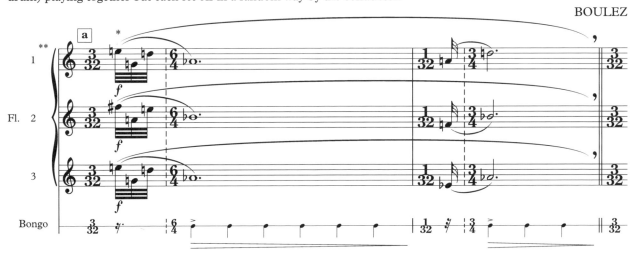

*the demi-semiquaver preceding the long note should always be very quick
**the instrument assumes the rôle of leader of his group

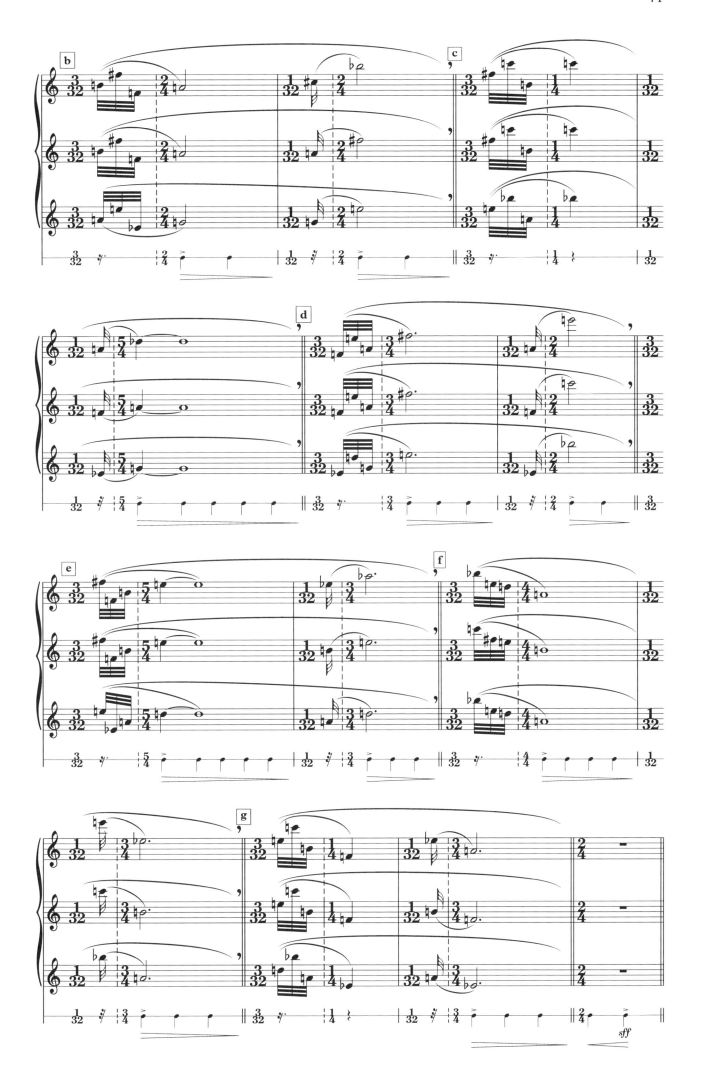

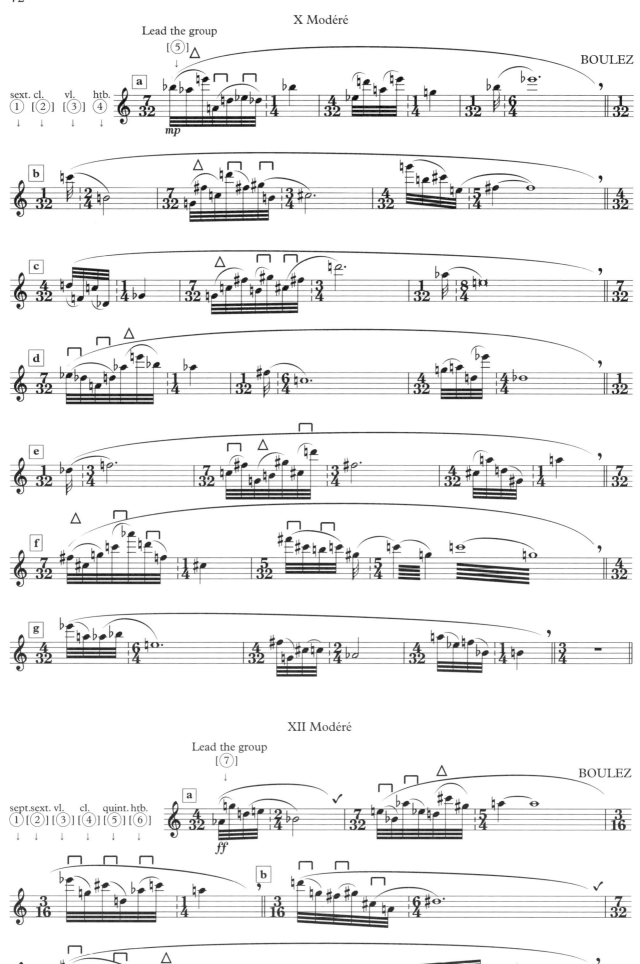

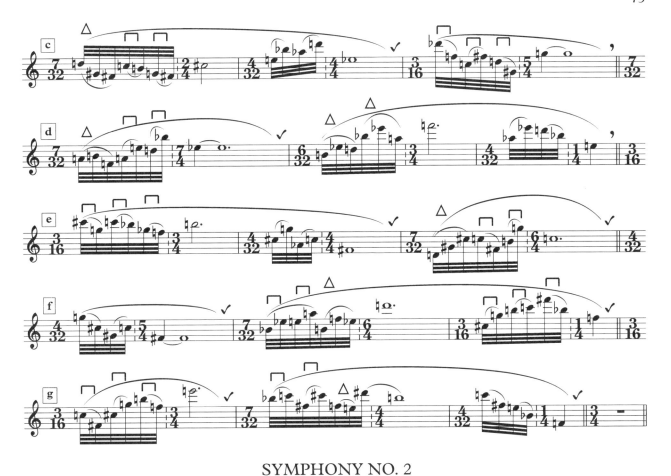

SYMPHONY NO. 2

2nd Movement

This entire passage is a duet with the bassoon. The first line is given as a cue.

MAXWELL DAVIES

SYMPHONY NO. 1

(Revised Version 1963 for Chamber Orchestra)

1st Movement

HENZE

2nd Movement: Notturno

3rd Movement

* Hs = Hauptstimme (main part)   ** hervor = from behind

THREE PLACES IN NEW ENGLAND

II Putman's Camp, Redding, Connecticut

IVES

LONTANO

The composer's experiments with orchestral colour require control of dynamics, breathing and tone far in excess of the demands of more classical repertoire.

Sostenuto espressivo ($\quad$ = 64)

LIGETI

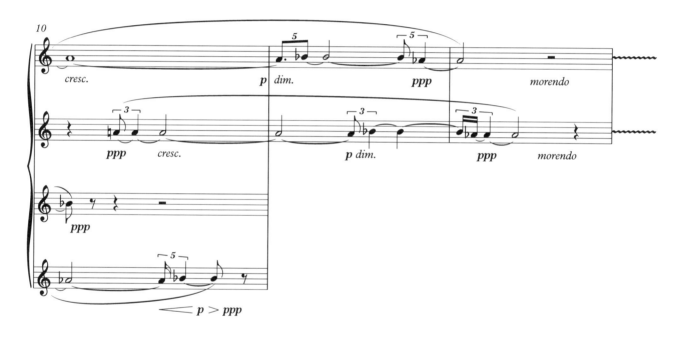

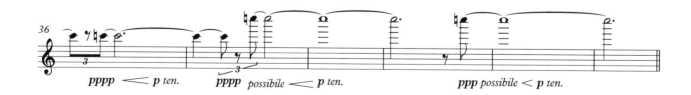

JEUX VENITIENS

III

What a relief to be given some freedom from the bar lines! But, as you will see from the instructions, it must fit in.
Practise this to achieve an expressive solo, creating a sensation of extemporisation and freedom within the limits set.

LUTOSŁAWSKI

CHRONOCHROMIE

STROPHE I

These are just a few of the bird calls to illustrate the composer's very specific notation.

STROPHE II

(3 bars tacet)

OISEAUX EXOTIQUES

MESSIAEN

PIERROT LUNAIRE

Melodrama for a speaker and five instrumentalists, Op. 21

Part i: 1. Mondestrunken

[for flute, viola, piano, cello and speaker]

SCHOENBERG

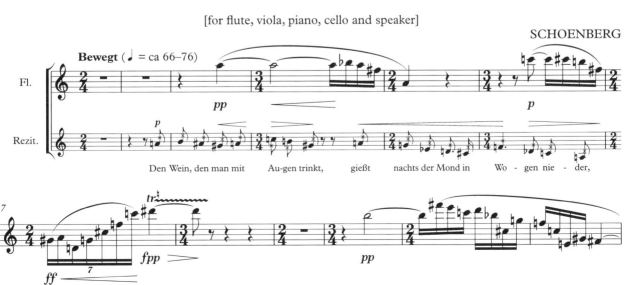

5. Valse de Chopin

7. Der kranke Mond

[flute and speaker]

Du näch - tig to - des-kran-ker Mond dort auf des Him - mels schwar - zem

Pfühl, dein Blick, so fie - bernd ü - ber-groß,

bannt mich, wie frem - de Me -lo - die.

An un - still - ba - ram Lie - bes - leid stirbst

du, an Sehn-sucht, tief er - stickst, du näch - tig to - des-kran-ker

Mond, dort auf des Him - mels schwar-zem Pfühl.

Den Lieb - sten, der im Sin-nen-rausch_ ge-dan-ken-los zur Lieb-sten geht, be - lu-stigt deiner Strah-len Spiel, dein

(im Ton genauso wie der vorhergehende Takt)   *(dieser Takt anders, aber doch nicht tragisch!!)*

blei-ches, qual-ge - bor-nes Blut, du näch - tig to - des-kran - ker Mond!

Part iii. 20. Heimfahrt

(Barcarole)

Leicht bewegt (♩. = 42–46)

KONTRA-PUNKTE

STOCKHAUSEN

HYPERPRISM

VARESE

FÜNF GEISTLICHE LIEDER, OP. 15

(For voice, flute, clarinet doubling bass clarinet, trumpet, harp and violin doubling viola)

WEBERN

I. Das Kreuz

IV. Mein Weg geht jetzt vorüber

General Section

We have added some helpful notes where appropriate. We leave the rest to you!

PIANO CONCERTO NO. 1 IN F♯ MINOR

2nd Movement

RACHMANINOV

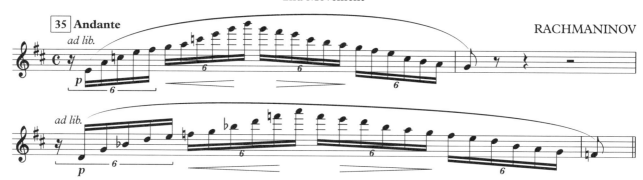

PIANO CONCERTO NO. 2 IN C MINOR

2nd Movement

Be careful of intonation in this exposed solo, and take a breath before it!

RACHMANINOV

RHAPSODY ON A THEME OF PAGANINI

for piano and orchestra

Variation III

This has to be louder than *piano* to cut through the texture.

RACHMANINOV

Variation XX

SYMPHONY NO. 2 IN E MINOR

2nd Movement

RACHMANINOV

3rd Movement

4th Movement

SYMPHONY NO. 3 IN A MINOR

1st Movement

RACHMANINOV

SYMPHONIC DANCES

No. 1

1st Movement

RACHMANINOV

3rd Movement

DAPHNIS ET CHLOÉ

1st Suite

Nocturne – Interlude – Danse Guerrière

RAVEL

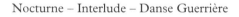

As the 2nd flute often plays alto in this piece, freelancers are frequently required to play the 2nd flute part. We recommend you learn this tricky part, ready for the invitation!

2nd Suite

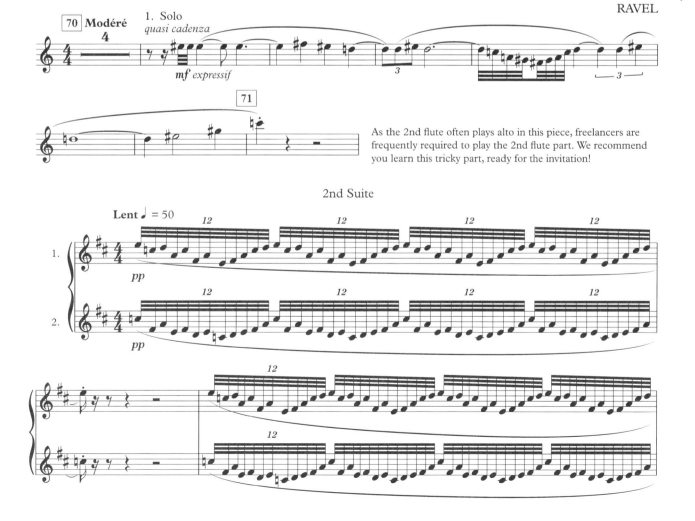

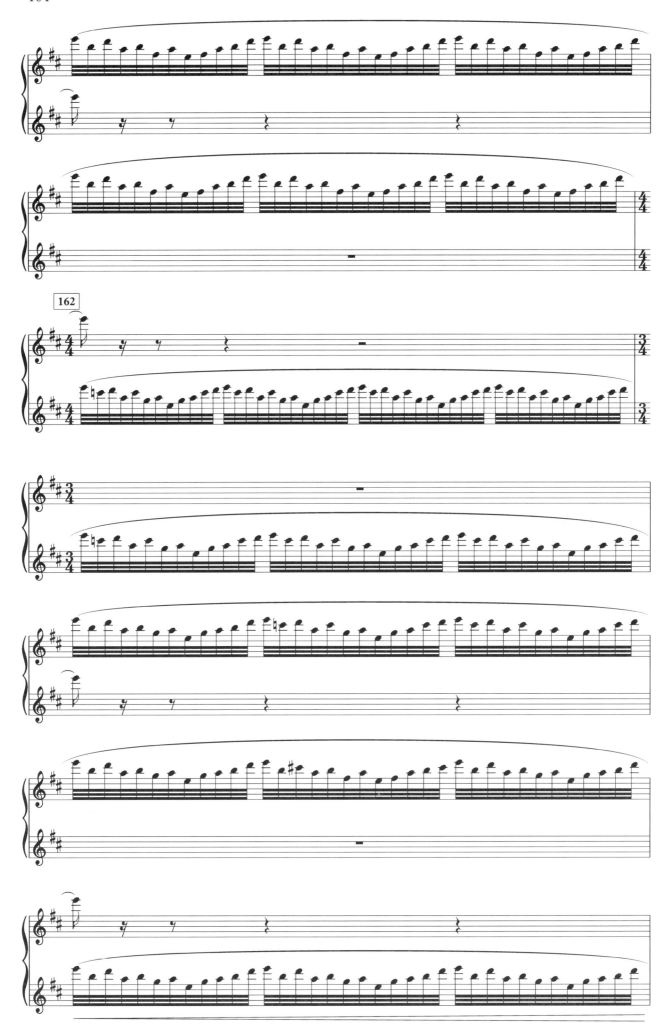

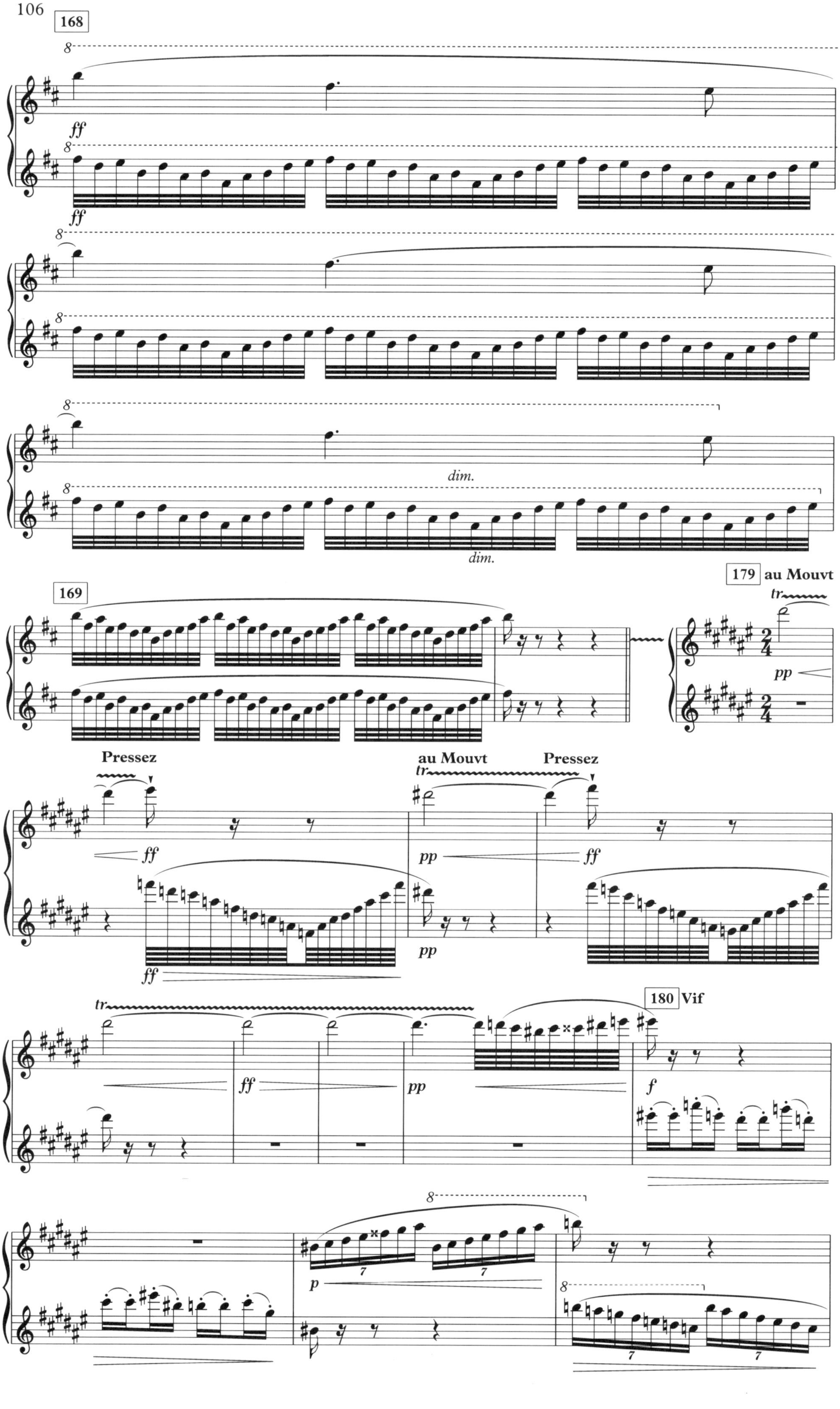
168
8
ff
ff
8
8
8
8
dim.
dim.
179 au Mouvt
169
tr
pp
Pressez
au Mouvt
Pressez
tr
ff
pp
ff
pp
ff
tr
180 Vif
ff
pp
f
8
p
7
7
8
7
7

MA MÈRE L'OYE

Suite2

III Laideronnette, Impératrice des Pagodes

RAVEL

SHÉHÉRAZADE

II La flûte enchantée

RAVEL

* An easier way to play this passage at speed is to finger A♯, B and C♯ in the middle register and overblow a fifth higher.

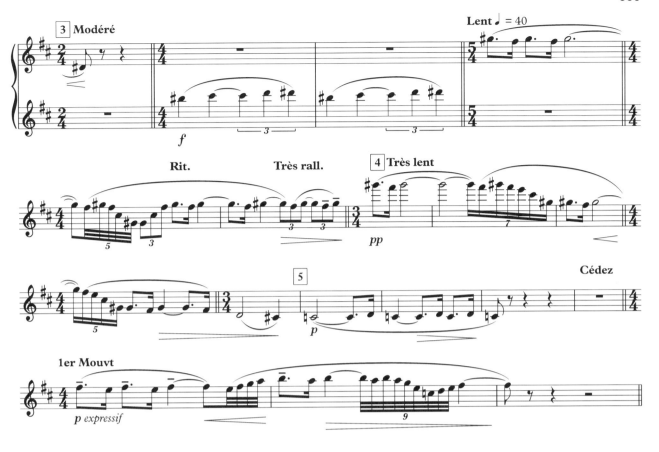

LA BOUTIQUE FANTASQUE

Tarantella

RESPIGHI, after ROSSINI

Danse Cosaque

Valse Lente

Vivacissimo (♩ = 176)

Galop

Allegro brillante

Prestissimo

FESTE ROMANE

I. Circenses

RESPIGHI

Molto allegro ♩. = 80

1. & 2.

Allegro vivo ♩ = 100

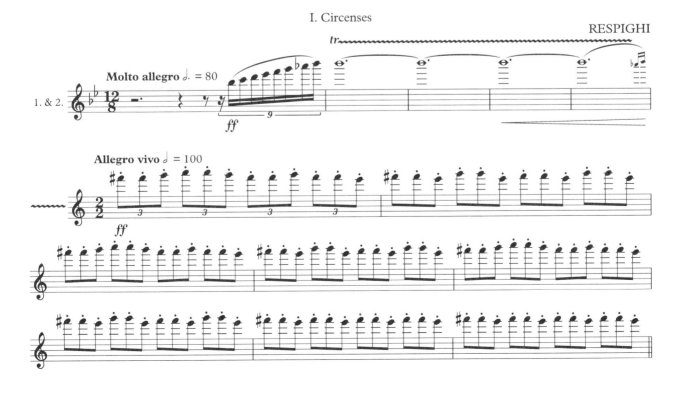

III. L'ottobrata

IV. La Befana

FONTANE DI ROMA

1. La fontana di Valle Giulia all'alba

RESPIGHI

2. La fontana del Tritone al mattino

3. La fontana di Trevi al meriggio

116

14 Più vivace
(Ritmo di 3 misure) (in uno)

(b)

a2

più f

4. La fontana di Villa Medici al tramonto

18 Andante ♩ = 72

p espress.

p

p

p *dim.*

ppp

PINI DI ROMA

I. I Pini di Villa Borghese

RESPIGHI

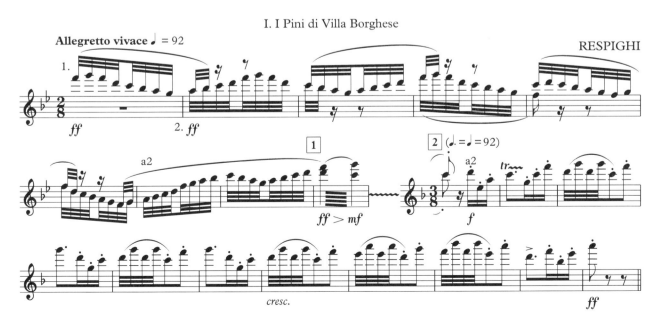

II. I Pini del Gianiculo

TRITTICO BOTTICELLIANO

I. La Primavera

RESPIGHI

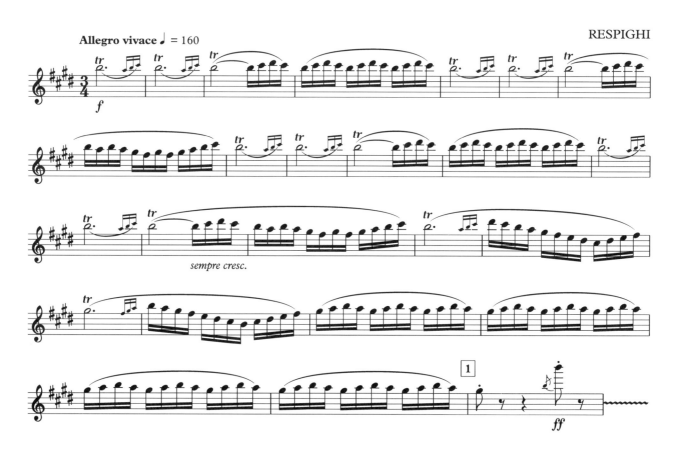

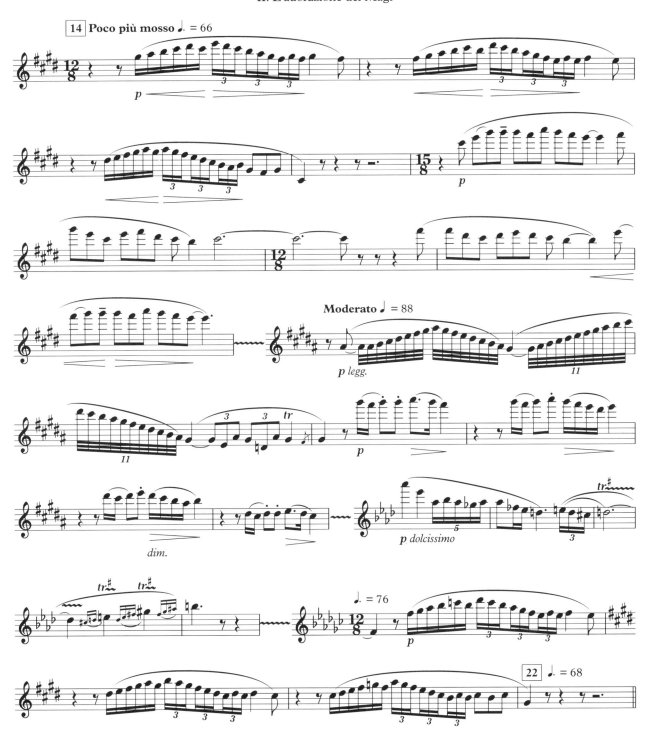

II. L'adorazione dei Magi

III. La nascita di Venere

GLI UCCELLI SUITE

(The Birds)

I. Preludio

RESPIGHI

II. La Colomba

III. La Gallina

IV. L'usignuolo

LE COQ D'OR

Suite

I.

RIMSKY-KORSAKOV

IV.

CAPRICCIO ESPAGNOL

I. Alborada

RIMSKY-KORSAKOV

II. Variazioni

IV. Scena e canto gitano

V. Fandango asturiano

SHEHERAZADE

1st Movement

RIMSKY-KORSAKOV

2nd Movement

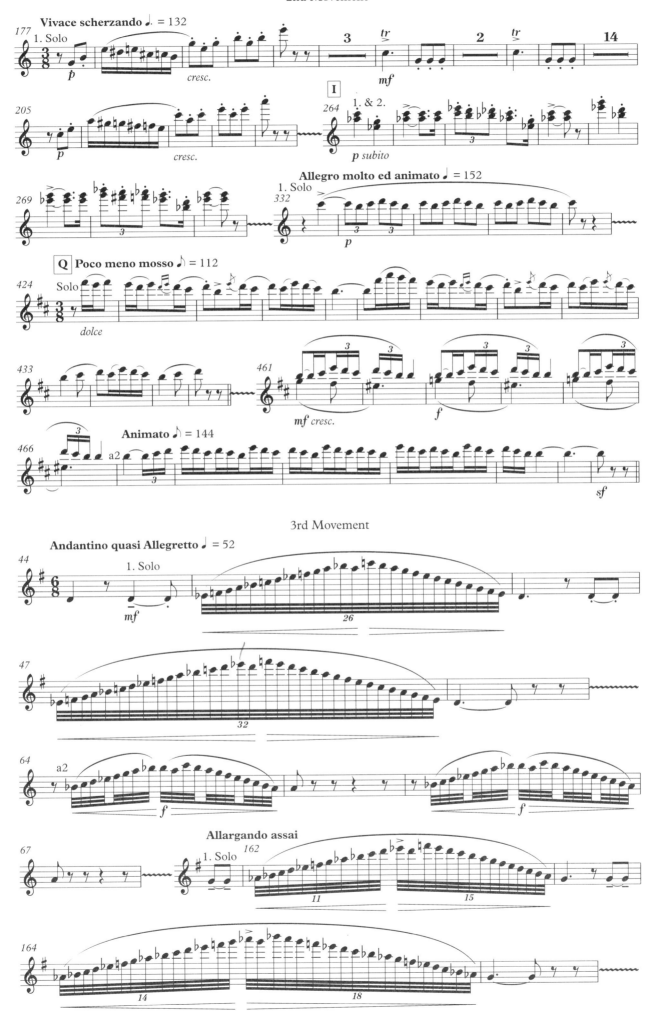

3rd Movement

4th Movement

IL BARBIERE DI SIVIGLIA

Overture

ROSSINI

No. 2 Cavatina: Largo al factotum

L'ITALIANA IN ALGERI

Overture

ROSSINI

IL TURCO IN ITALIA

Overture

ROSSINI

LE FESTIN DE L'ARAIGNÉE

ROUSSEL

CHAMBER SYMPHONY NO. 1, OP. 9

SCHOENBERG

GURRELIEDER

1st Part

SCHOENBERG

Des Sommerwindes wilde Jagd

134

These look simple but they need controlled playing, a clear tone and meticulous phrasing.

SYMPHONY NO. 4 IN C MINOR

The Tragic

2nd Movement

SCHUBERT

3rd Movement

4th Movement

SYMPHONY NO. 5 IN B♭ MAJOR

1st Movement

SCHUBERT

2nd Movement

3rd Movement

4th Movement

SYMPHONY NO. 6 IN C MAJOR

1st Movement

SCHUBERT

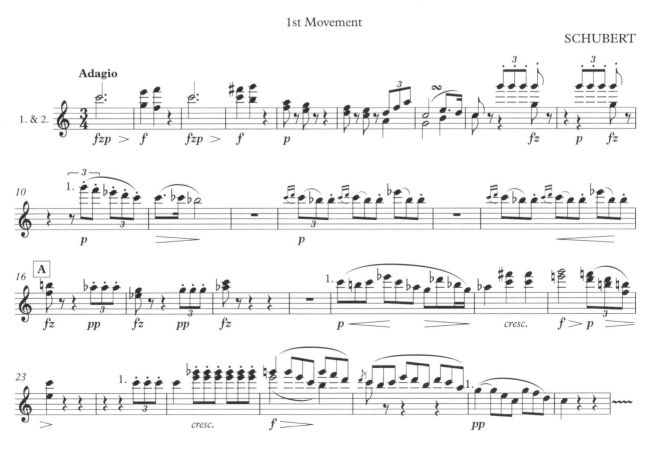

2nd Movement

4th Movement

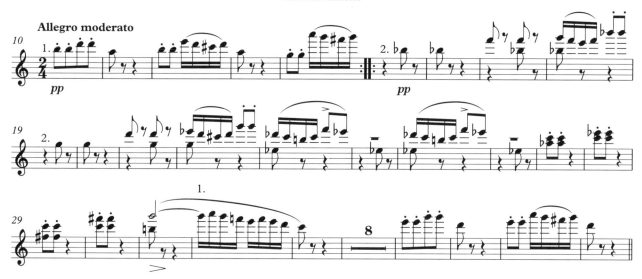

SYMPHONY NO. 8 IN B MINOR

'The Unfinished'

SCHUBERT

2nd Movement

SYMPHONY NO. 9 IN C MAJOR

'The Great'

1st Movement

SCHUBERT

2nd Movement

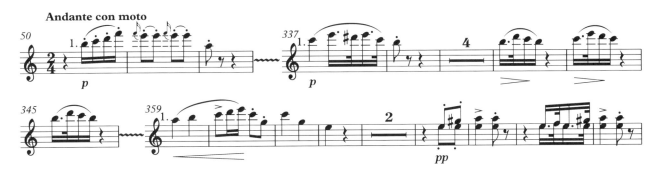

3rd Movement

SYMPHONY NO. 4 IN D MINOR

1st Movement

SCHUMANN

SYMPHONY NO. 1 IN F MINOR

1st Movement

SHOSTAKOVICH

3rd Movement

4th Movement

SYMPHONY NO. 4 IN C MINOR

1st Movement

SHOSTAKOVICH

2nd Movement

3rd Movement

SYMPHONY NO. 5 IN D MINOR

1st Movement

SHOSTAKOVICH

3rd Movement

4th Movement

SYMPHONY NO. 6 IN B MINOR

1st Movement

SHOSTAKOVICH

2nd Movement

3rd Movement

SYMPHONY NO. 7 IN C MAJOR

'The Leningrad'

1st Movement

SHOSTAKOVICH

4th Movement

SYMPHONY NO. 8 IN C MINOR

1st Movement

SHOSTAKOVICH

2nd Movement

5th Movement

2nd Movement

SYMPHONY NO. 9 IN Eb MAJOR

1st Movement

SHOSTAKOVICH

2nd Movement

SYMPHONY NO. 10 IN E MINOR

1st Movement

SHOSTAKOVICH

3rd Movement

4th Movement

SYMPHONY NO. 11 IN G MINOR

'The year 1905'

1st Movement: Palace Square

SHOSTAKOVICH

2nd Movement: Ninth of January

4th Movement

SYMPHONY NO. 15 IN A MAJOR

1st Movement

SHOSTAKOVICH

4th Movement

SYMPHONY NO. 4 IN A MINOR

3rd Movement

SIBELIUS

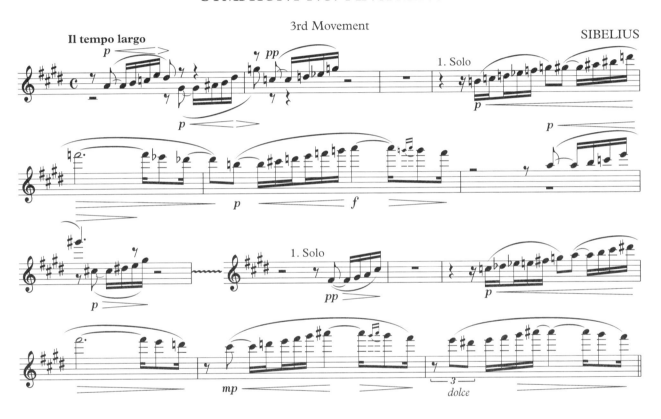

SYMPHONY NO. 5 IN E♭ MAJOR

1st Movement

SIBELIUS

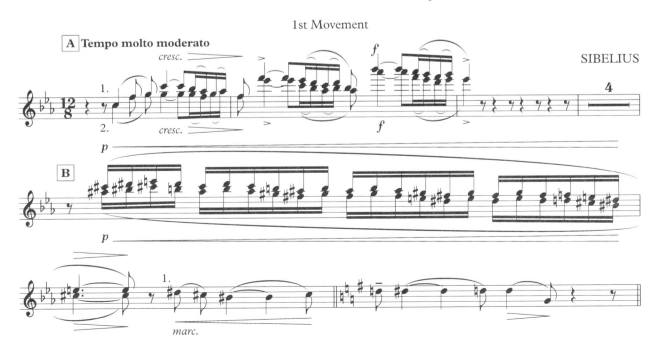

158

AN DER SCHÖNEN, BLAUEN DONAU, OP. 314

The Blue Danube Waltz

Introduction

JOHANN STRAUSS *the younger*
(1825–99)

Waltz No. 2

DIE FLEDERMAUS

Overture

JOHANN STRAUSS *the younger*

PERPETUUM MOBILE, OP. 257

JOHANN STRAUSS *the younger*

LE BAISER DE LA FÉE

(1928, rev. 1949)

Prologue

STRAVINSKY

CAPRICCIO

for piano and orchestra (1929, rev. 1949)

1st Movement

STRAVINSKY

2nd Movement

3rd Movement

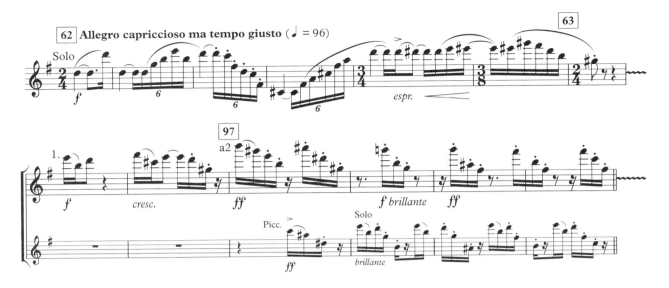

CHANT DU ROSSIGNOL

(Song of the Nightingale)

STRAVINSKY

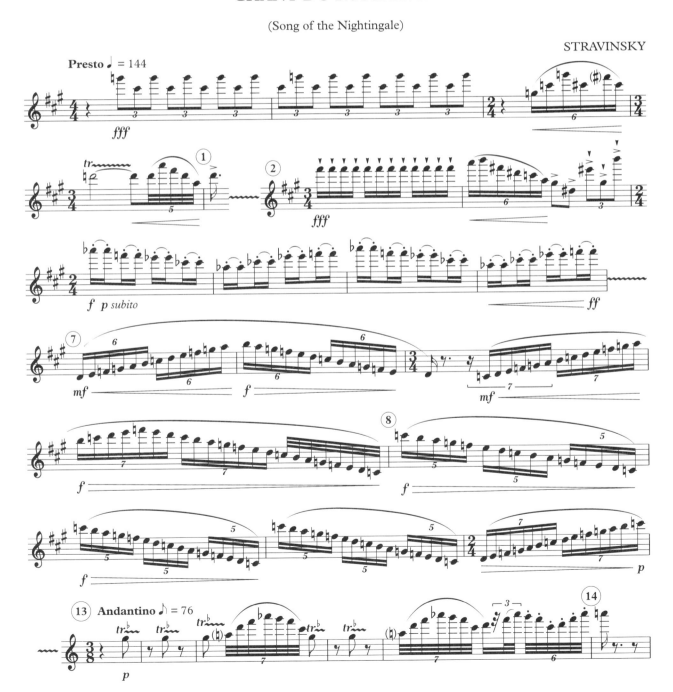

CIRCUS POLKA

STRAVINSKY

JEU DE CARTES

(The Card Party)

Première Donne

STRAVINSKY

164

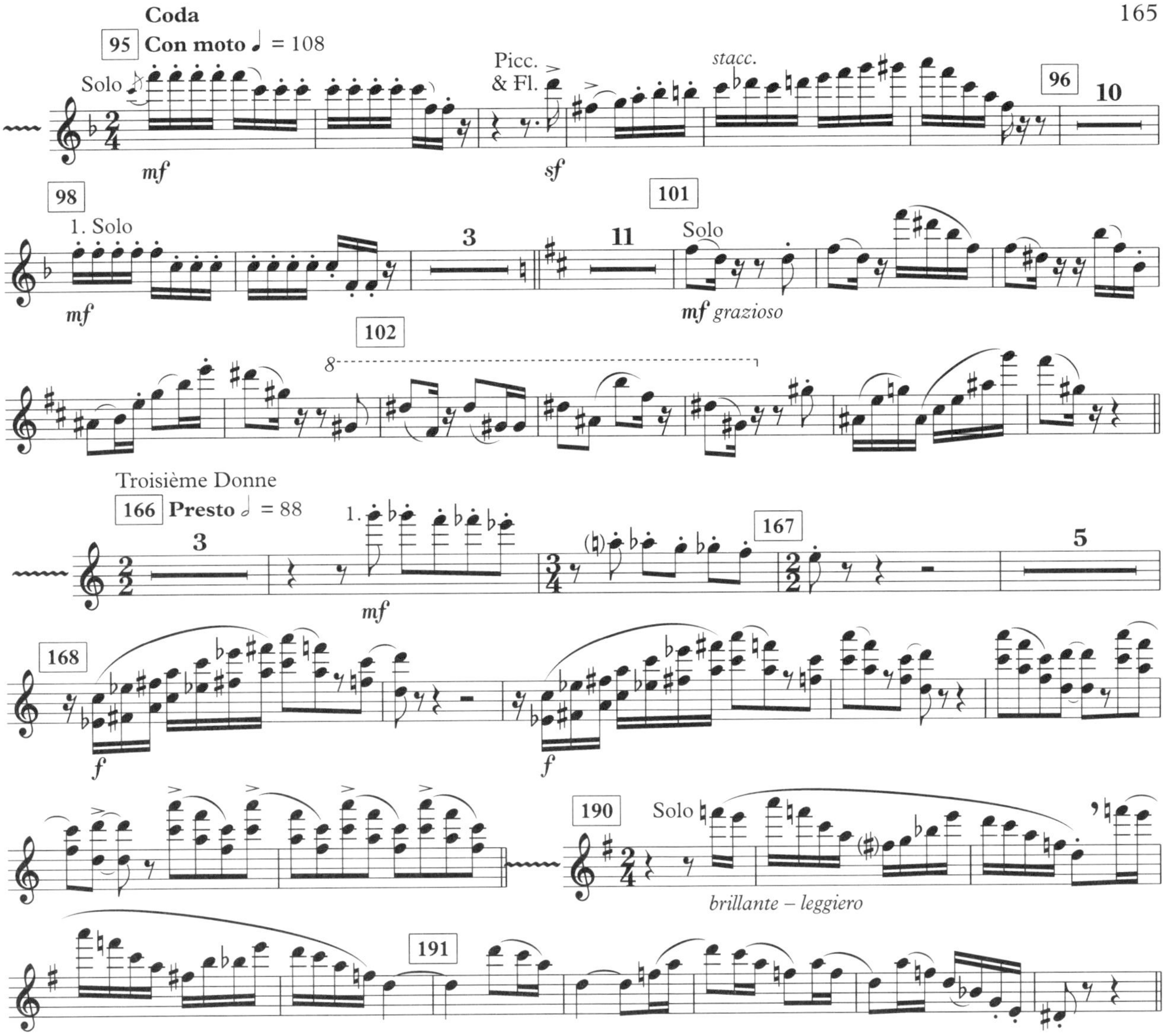

L'OISEAU DE FEU

(The Firebird: Ballet)

STRAVINSKY

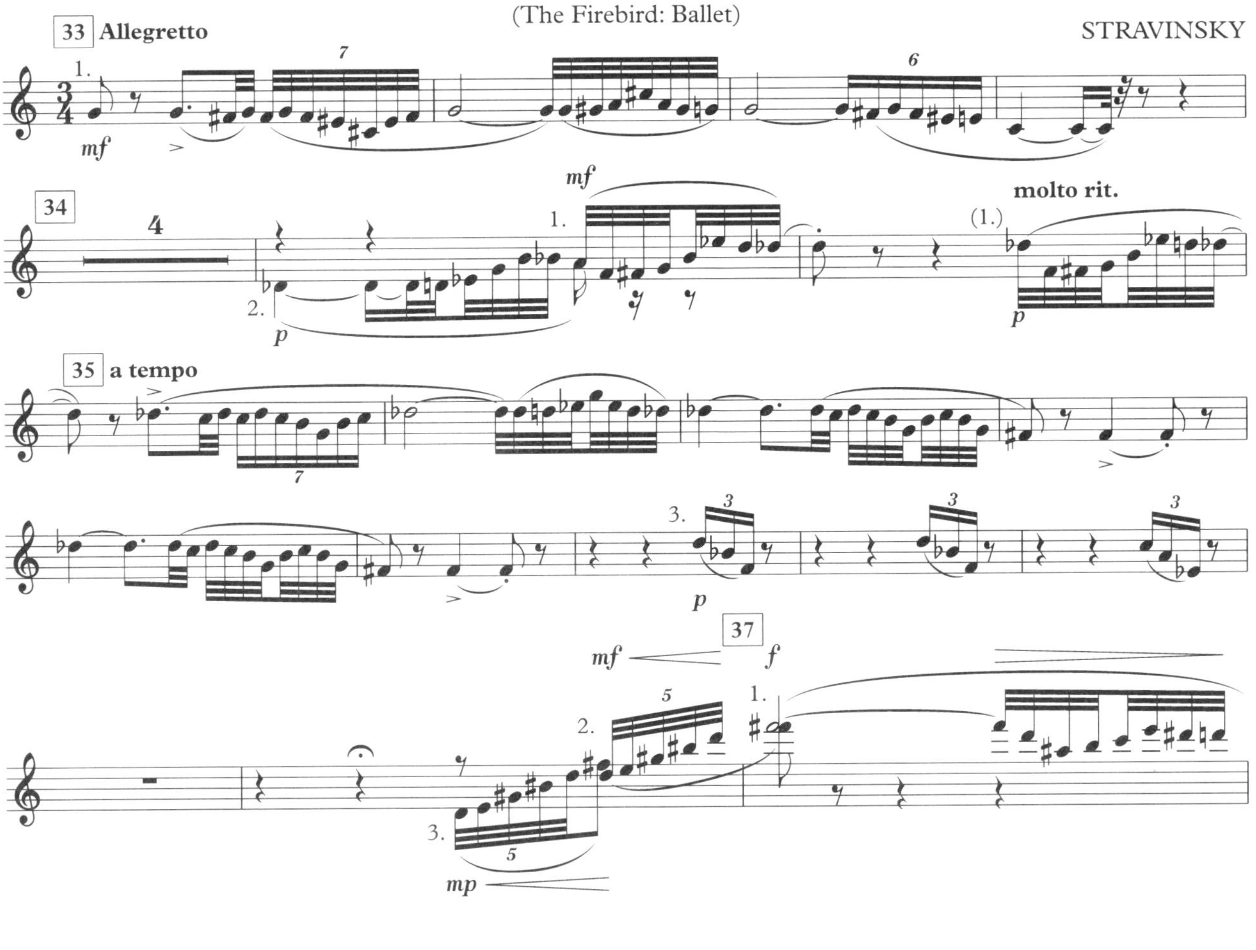

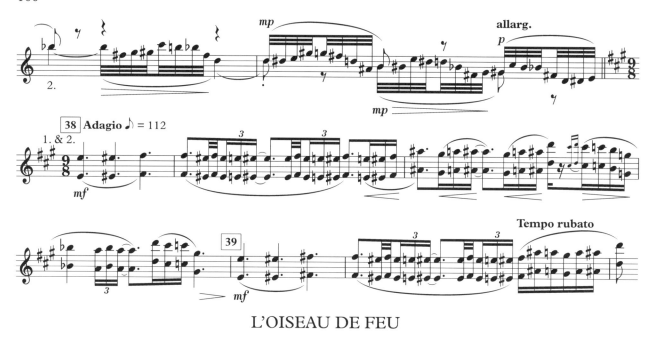

L'OISEAU DE FEU

(The Firebird: Suite, 1919)

Variation de l'oiseau de feu

STRAVINSKY

Ronde des princesses

Danse infernale du roi Kastcheï

PERSÉPHONE

1934, Revised 1949

I. Perséphone ravie

STRAVINSKY

II. Perséphone aux enfers

170

PETRUSHKA

1911 Version

Premier Tableau: Carnaval

STRAVINSKY

Le tour de passe-passe: Charlatan joue de la flûte

Danse de la Ballerine

Valse

(La ballerine et Arap)

PULCINELLA

(Revised 1965)

STRAVINSKY

Tarantella

Gavotta con due variazione

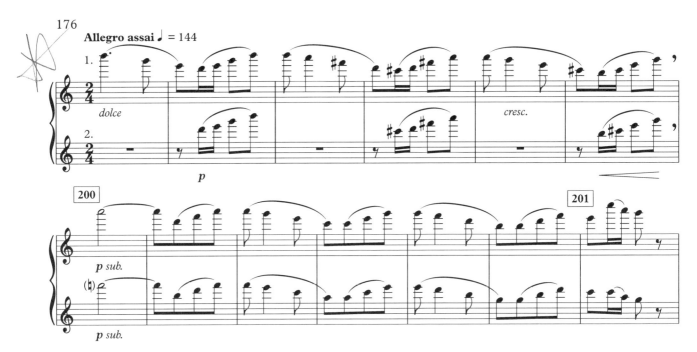

SYMPHONY IN C

1st Movement

STRAVINSKY

2nd Movement

3rd Movement

SYMPHONY OF PSALMS

(1948 revised version)

2nd Movement

STRAVINSKY

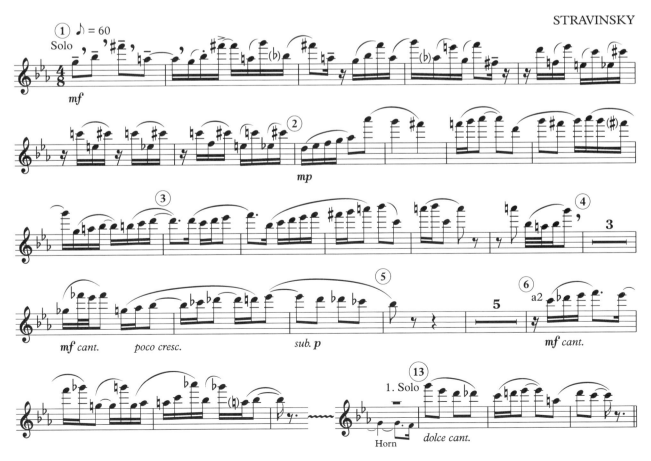

3rd Movement

OVERTURE DI BALLO

SULLIVAN

PIANO CONCERTO NO. 1 IN B♭ MINOR

1st Movement

TCHAIKOVSKY

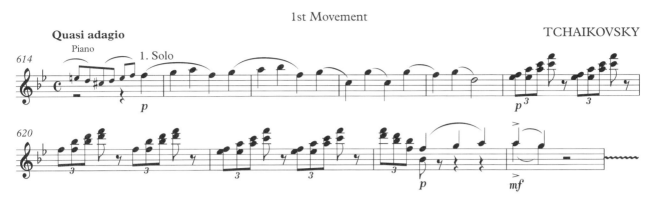

2nd Movement

3rd Movement

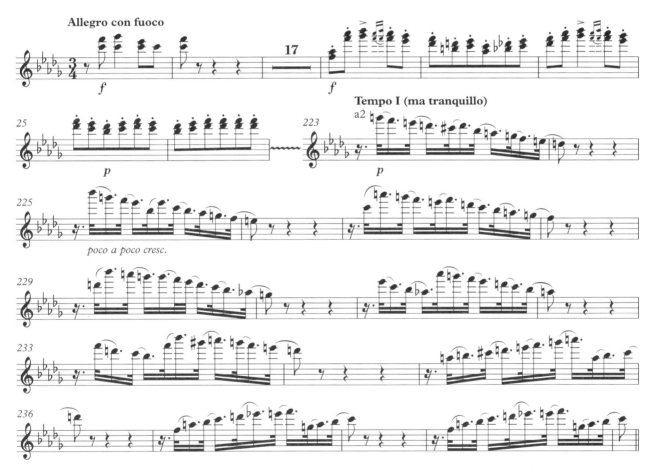

VIOLIN CONCERTO IN D MAJOR

1st Movement

TCHAIKOVSKY

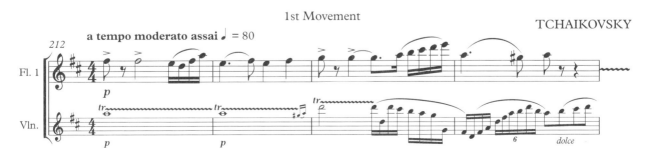

FRANCESCA DA RIMINI

Symphonic Fantasia

TCHAIKOVSKY

MANFRED

Symphony

1st Movement

TCHAIKOVSKY

2nd Movement

3rd Movement

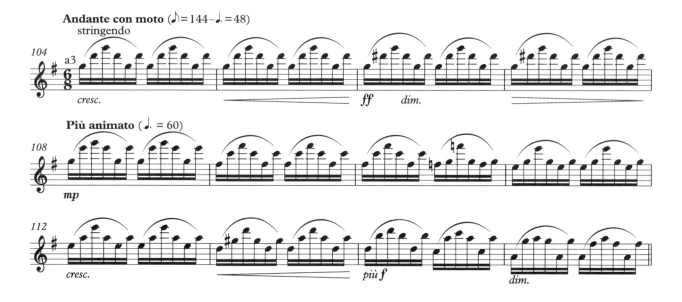

4th Movement

THE NUTCRACKER

Suite

I Ouverture miniature

TCHAIKOVSKY

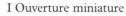

IIe Danse Chinoise

The trill will need to be properly supported for the G to be in tune.

IIf Danse des Mirlitons

THE SLEEPING BEAUTY

Prologue: (Pas de six) Canari qui chante

TCHAIKOVSKY

SUITE NO. 3

IV Theme and variations

Var. I

TCHAIKOVSKY

Var. IX

E Allegro molto vivace ♩ = 152

F Più presto

Cadenza

SUITE NO. 4 IN G MAJOR

'Mozartiana'

IV. Thème et Variations

Var. III

Allegro giusto

TCHAIKOVSKY

Var. VI

SYMPHONY NO. 4 IN F MINOR

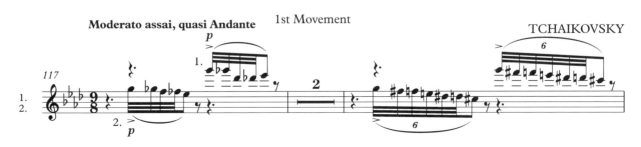

Moderato assai, quasi Andante   1st Movement

TCHAIKOVSKY

2nd Movement

Andantino in modo di canzona

3rd Movement

4th Movement

SYMPHONY NO. 5 IN E MINOR

3rd Movement

TCHAIKOVSKY

4th Movement

Finale

MIGNON

Overture

THOMAS

Moderato, tempo di Polacca (♩ = 100)

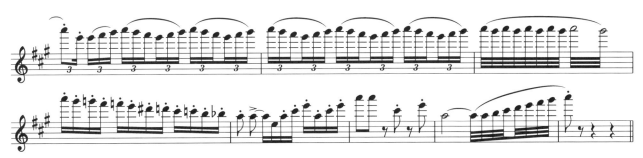

* This special fingering for a *pianissimo* top B♭ is known as the 'Mignon' fingering.

THE MIDSUMMER MARRIAGE

Ritual Dances

Prelude

TIPPETT

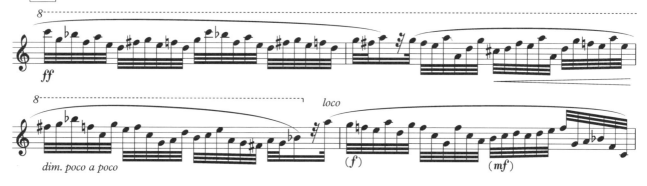

First Dance. The earth in autumn.

Second Dance. The waters in winter.

Con un poco moto, agitato e marc.

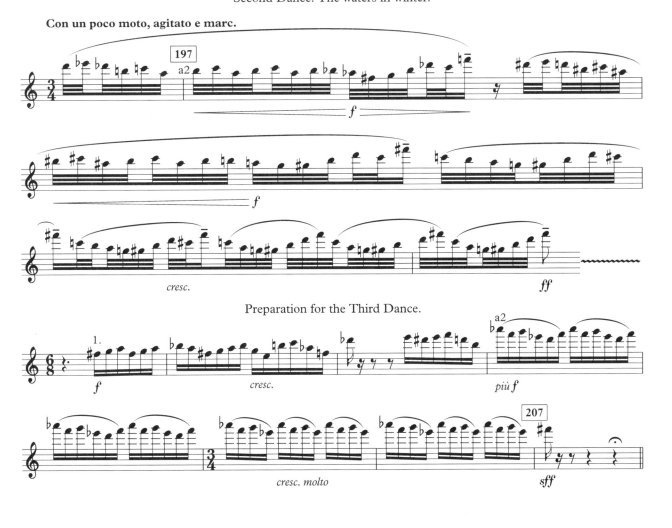

Preparation for the Third Dance.

Third Dance. The air in spring.

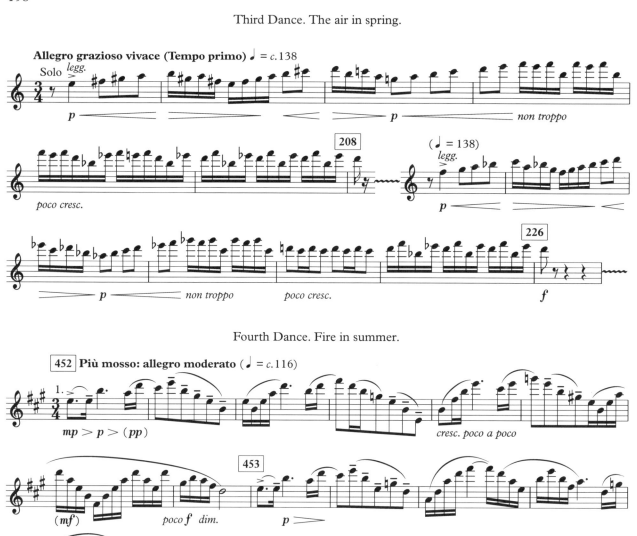

Fourth Dance. Fire in summer.

THE SICILIAN VESPERS

Overture

VERDI

SYMPHONY NO. 4 IN F MINOR

2nd Movement

VAUGHAN WILLIAMS

SYMPHONY NO. 6 IN E MINOR

1st Movement

VAUGHAN WILLIAMS

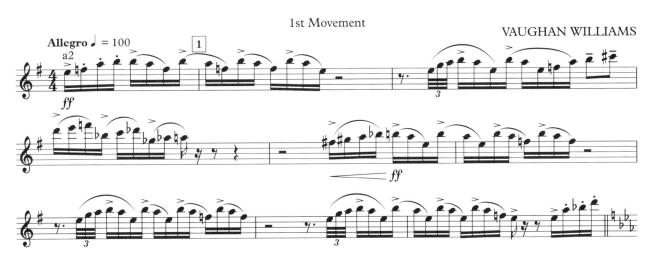

200

3rd Movement: Scherzo

4th Movement: Epilogue

SIEGFRIED

Waldweben. (Forest Murmurs)

WAGNER

FAÇADE

Suite No. 1

I Polka

WALTON

II Valse

V Tarantella Sevillana

FAÇADE

Suite No. 2

II. Scotch Rhapsody

WALTON

IV. Noche Espagnola

V. Popular Song

Grazioso

VI. Old Sir Faulk

Tempo di Fox Trot

SCAPINO

Overture

WALTON

Molto vivace ♩ = c.138

ABU HASSAN

Overture

WEBER

EURYANTHE

Overture

WEBER

DER FREISCHÜTZ

Overture

WEBER

OBERON

Overture

WEBER

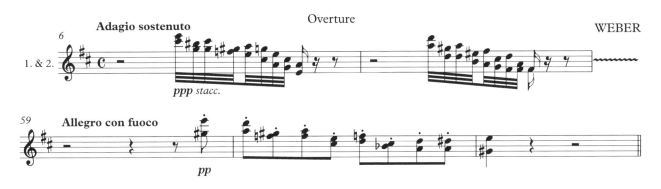

* Although written at the lower 8ve, this is often played an 8ve higher.

INVITATION TO THE DANCE

(Aufforderung zum Tanze)

WEBER
Orch. Berlioz

THE JEWELS OF THE MADONNA

Intermezzo No. 2

Introduction to Act 3

WOLF-FERRARI

LYRISCHE SYMPHONIE

1st Movement

ZEMLINSKY

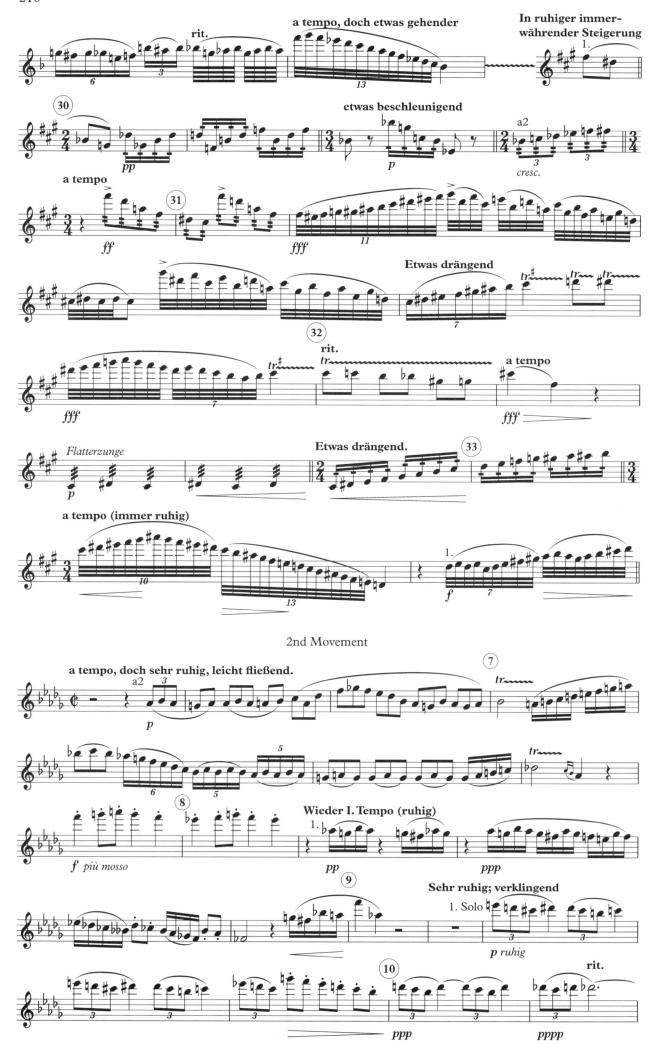

2nd Movement

Etwas gehaltener, doch immer leidenschaftlich bewegt.

5th Movement

7th Movement

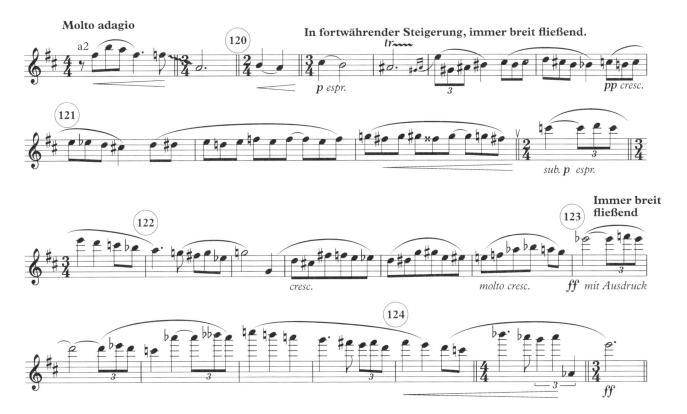

INDEX

ACKNOWLEDGEMENTS

Extracts from the following works are reprinted by permission of the publishers concerned. (We have endeavoured to trace all copyright holders but will be pleased to rectify any omissions notified to us in future reprints.)

Berg   Kammerkonzert — Copyright 1925 by Universal Edition. Copyright renewed 1953 by Helene Berg.

Berg   Violin Concerto — Copyright 1936 by Universal Edition. Copyright renewed 1964.

Berio   Laborintus II — © Copyright 1976 by Universal Edition S. p. A., Milano.

Birtwistle   Nomos — © Copyright 1971 by Universal Edition (London) Ltd., London.

Boulez   Rituel in Memoriam Bruno Maderna — © 1975 by Universal Edition (London) Ltd., London.

Britten   The Young Person's Guide to the Orchestra — © Copyright 1946 by Hawkes & Son (London) Ltd. Reproduced by permission of Boosey & Hawkes Music Publishers Ltd.

Delius   Brigg Fair — © Copyright 1910, 1911 by F.E.C. Leuckart, Leipzig; Renewed 1938. Copyright assigned 1921 to Universal Edition. Renewal copyright assigned to Boosey & Hawkes, Inc. 1943. Revised edition © Copyright 1953 by Boosey & Hawkes, Inc. Second Revised Edition © Copyright 1989 by Universal Edition (London) Ltd., London.

Henze   Symphony No.1 — © 1992 B. Schott's Söhne, Mainz.

Ives   Three Places in New England — © 1935 by Mercury Music Corp., Bryn Mawr, Pa. Copyright renewed. Theodore Presser Co., Sole Representative.

Kodály   Variations on a Hungarian Folksong — © 1941, 1957 by Hawkes & Son (London) Ltd. For the World excluding Hungary. Reproduced by permission of Boosey & Hawkes Music Publishers Ltd.

Ligeti   Lontano — © B. Schott's Söhne, Mainz, 1969.

Lutoslawski   Jeux Venitiens — © Copyright by MOECK VERLAG UND MUSIKINSTRUMENTENWERK, D-Celle.

Maxwell Davies   Symphony No.2 — © Copyright 1978 by Boosey & Hawkes Music Publishers Ltd. Reproduced by permission of Boosey & Hawkes Music Publishers Ltd.

Messiaen   Chronochromie — Reproduced by permission of Editions Alphonse Leduc/United Music Publishers Ltd.

Messiaen   Oiseaux Exotiques — © Copyright 1959 by Universal Edition (London) Ltd., London.

Rachmaninov   Piano Concerto No.1 — © Copyright 1919 by Hawkes & Son (London) Ltd. Reproduced by permission of Boosey & Hawkes Music Publishers Ltd.

Rachmaninov   Piano Concerto No.2 — © Copyright 1901 by Hawkes & Son (London) Ltd. Reproduced by permission of Boosey & Hawkes Music Publishers Ltd.

Rachmaninov   Rhapsody on a Theme of Paganini — © 1934 EMI Mills Music Inc, USA. Worldwide print rights controlled by Warner Bros Publications Inc/IMP Ltd. Used by permission of International Music Publications Limited, Woodford Green, Essex IG8 8HN.

Rachmaninov   Symphonic Dances — © 1942 EMI Mills Music Inc, USA. Worldwide print rights controlled by Warner Bros Publications Inc/IMP Ltd. Used by permission of International Music Publications Limited, Woodford Green, Essex IG8 8HN.

Rachmaninov   Symphony No.2 — © Copyright 1908 by Hawkes & Son (London) Ltd. Reproduced by permission of Boosey & Hawkes Music Publishers Ltd.